The Oil
21-Day
Devotional Journal

Bridgett McGill
Sharon Gilchrist

The Queen Within LLC
Chicago, Illinois

Edited by Janice M. Allen http://www.naleighnakai.com
Cover Designed by J.L Woodson: http://www.woodsoncreativestudio.com
Interior Designed by Lissa Woodson: http://www.naleighnakai.com

Dedication

This book is dedicated to every woman that has been a human vessel of oil in my life. Thank you for the oil of your words of wisdom, the oil of your prayers, the oil of your friendship. I am who I am because of the oil on your life that you poured into mine.

Bridgett McGill

This book is dedicated first to my Lord and Savior Jesus Christ from whom all blessings flow. To Bridgett McGill for believing in me and always encouraging me to do something new. To Shoshanna Faust, who started me on my physical oil journey. To every woman who encounters this journal, may your pressing create oil in abundance, and beyond measure! Peace & Love

Sharon Gilchrist

Bridgett and Sharon have collaborated on this journal to remind every woman of the oil she possesses. The Most High intended for His oil to flow freely with power, love and joy so that every woman may live and move in the highest version of herself.

Introduction

Why the Oil?

In recent years, there has been a surge in the use of essential oils. They are showing up everywhere from household cleaners to diffusers in hospital emergency rooms. It's no wonder oils are on the rise. They are from the earth and the Bible says:

Fruit trees of all kinds will grow on both banks of the river. Their leaves will not wither, nor will their fruit fail. Every month they will bear fruit, because the water from the sanctuary flows to them. Their fruit will serve for food and their leaves for healing." Ezekiel 47:12

The Lord is absolutely strategic in everything; not a single word in the scriptures is written without significance.

The word "oil" is mentioned in the Bible 191 times, so it's clearly important to The Most High God. As we read through the scripture, we find the oil represented in various forms. The Word of God can be a representation of the oil. The oil shows up in the form of the Holy Spirit. And the oil is most definitely represented in forms of human vessels.

Some of Jesus' last moments were spent in the Garden of Gethsemane. This garden was a small grove consisting of eight ancient olive trees at the foot of The Mount of Olives, right outside the city of Jerusalem.

In the middle of the garden was an oil press in which olive oil was made. The word Gethsemane is the Hebrew word for "olive press".

Isaiah writes of Jesus being crushed for our iniquities and his form marred beyond human likeness. Again, the Bible is written with countless metaphors and comparisons. The way a plant or fruit is crushed to produce oil is the same way Jesus was crushed to produce the oil of salvation. His body, marred beyond human likeness, can be compared to the skins of fruits that after pressing are dried and used as paper, having no resemblance to the fruit skin it originally was.

The Bible also speaks of a widow who had a "bit" of oil. After the prophet Elisha activated her oil with the words of oil from his mouth, the widow's oil flowed until there were no more jars to fill. What do we learn from her story? She already had everything she needed to resolve her debt; she had oil in her life. She couldn't see what she had because of the press or crush that was happening within the threat of her sons being taken away.

We all have "oil" in our lives because we were made in the image and likeness of The Most High. The pressing or crushing can come from internal or external occurrences. Our responsibility during the press is to let the oil flow. That happens when we respond not by focusing on the press; (for presses are inevitable), but focus on the oil.

The oil on our lives is a gift that we should love, cherish and respect. When we don't, there are consequences. We learn in Deuteronomy that the "oil" can slip through our hands because of disobedience or unwise choices.

You will have olive trees throughout your country but you will not use the oil, because the olives will drop off. Deuteronomy 28:40

My dear sisters, hold on to your oil. The Holy Spirit is the activation for the oil to bless us with the flow of life. Love your oil, believe in your oil and thank Yahweh for your oil every day.

Selah

Day 1

"Take the following fine spices: 500 shekels of liquid myrrh, half as much (that is, 250 shekels) of fragrant cinnamon, 250 shekels of fragrant calamus, 500 shekels of cassia—all according to the sanctuary shekel—and a hin of olive oil. Make these into a sacred anointing oil, a fragrant blend, the work of a perfumer. It will be the sacred anointing oil.

MEDITATION

There is a science to making oil. It is not just pressed from plants by happenstance. It requires using the right plants in the right amounts. The oil is real and powerful. Do you recognize the oil in your life?

What does the beauty of your unique oil look like?

Bergamot

SPIRITUAL MEANING: The oil of the rightful place.

ORIGIN:

Bergamot essential oil comes from a citrus fruit which grows on a tree native to Italy. This oil is extracted from the peel of the fruit through a cold-pressed method. It has been used to help treat Malaria and rid the body of intestinal worms.

BENEFITS:

Bergamot is used in many perfumes. It relieves stress and anxiety. It is used as a sleep remedy, anti-inflammatory and can be used for skin and hair.

BLENDS WITH:

Lavender, Patchouli, Frankincense, Cedarwood, Sandalwood, Rosemary, Eucalyptus, and Lemon.

DIFFUSER BLENDS:

Anxiety Relief Recipe
4 drops Lavender
4 drops Patchouli
4 drops Bergamot

Stress Less
3 drops Bergamot
2 drops Frankincense
2 drops Lavender

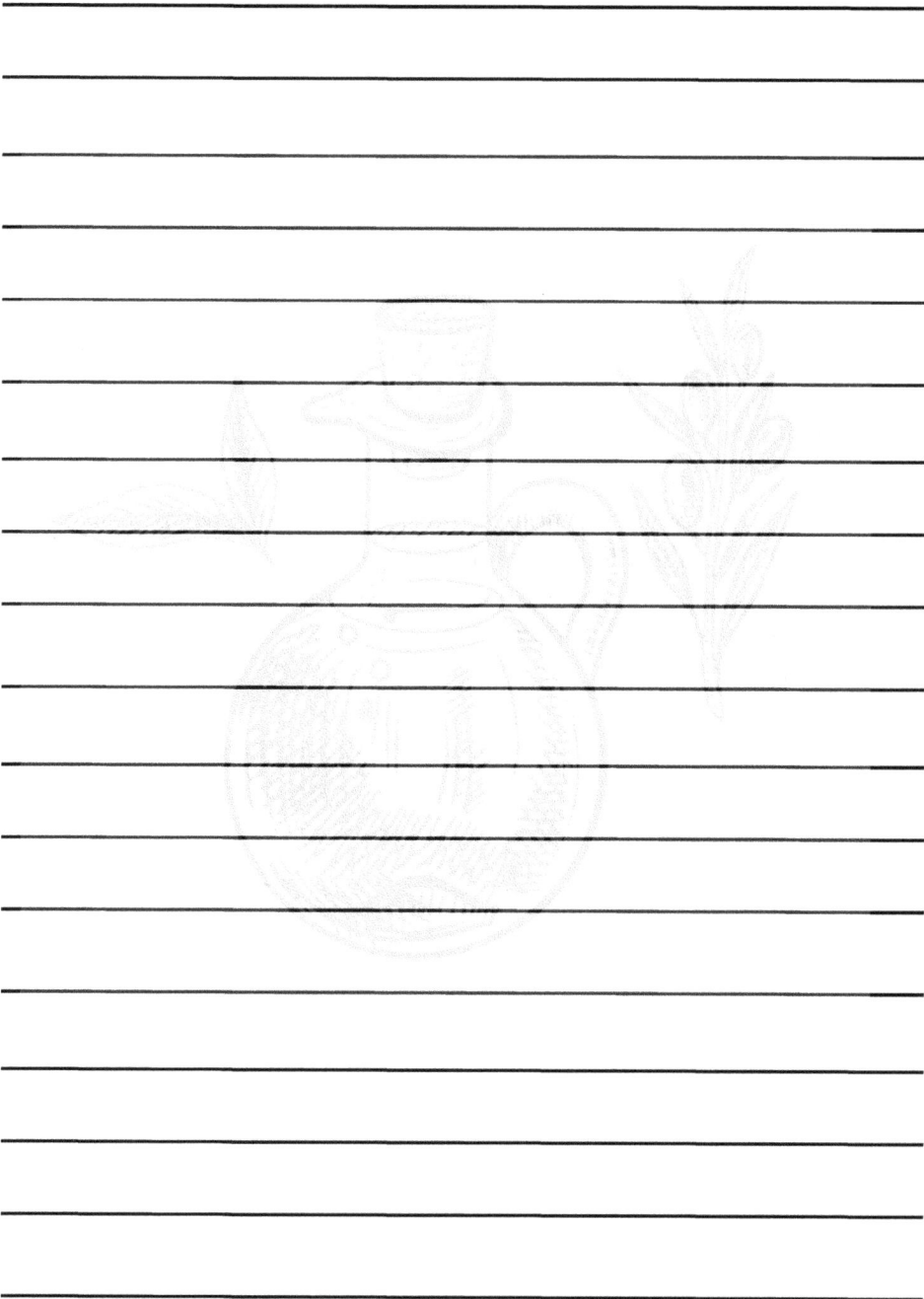

Day 2

Exodus 40: 9-11
 "Take the anointing oil and anoint the tabernacle and everything in it; consecrate it and all its furnishings, and it will be holy. 10 Then anoint the altar of burnt offering and all its utensils; consecrate the altar, and it will be most holy. 11 Anoint the basin and its stand and consecrate them.

MEDITATION

Today's Tabernacles are our bodies, our homes, our hearts (minds), where we work and other places we inhabit. The Oil of the Holy Spirit must be with us wherever we go. This oil is also physical oil that we use to manually anoint the various tabernacles. Most importantly we must anoint the tabernacles we inhabit with the oil of the Lord through our words and actions.

In what ways can you physically or verbally anoint your various tabernacles?

What's your favorite essential oil and why?

Cedarwood

SPIRITUAL MEANING: The oil of purification.

ORIGIN:

Cedarwood essential oil originates from the bark and wood pieces of the Cedar Tree, through the process of steam distillation. Native to North America, it has a woodsy aroma with sweet undertones that make it a great meditative oil.

BENEFITS:

Improves focus, anti-fungal, hair growth, anti-inflammatory.

BLENDS WITH:

Frankincense, Bergamot, Cinnamon, Lemon, Patchouli, Sandalwood, Lavender and Rosemary.

DIFFUSER BLENDS:

Ground & Focus
3 drops Cedarwood
3 drops Lemon
1 drop Rosemary

Stress Less
3 drops Cedarwood
2 drops Frankincense
2 drops Lavender

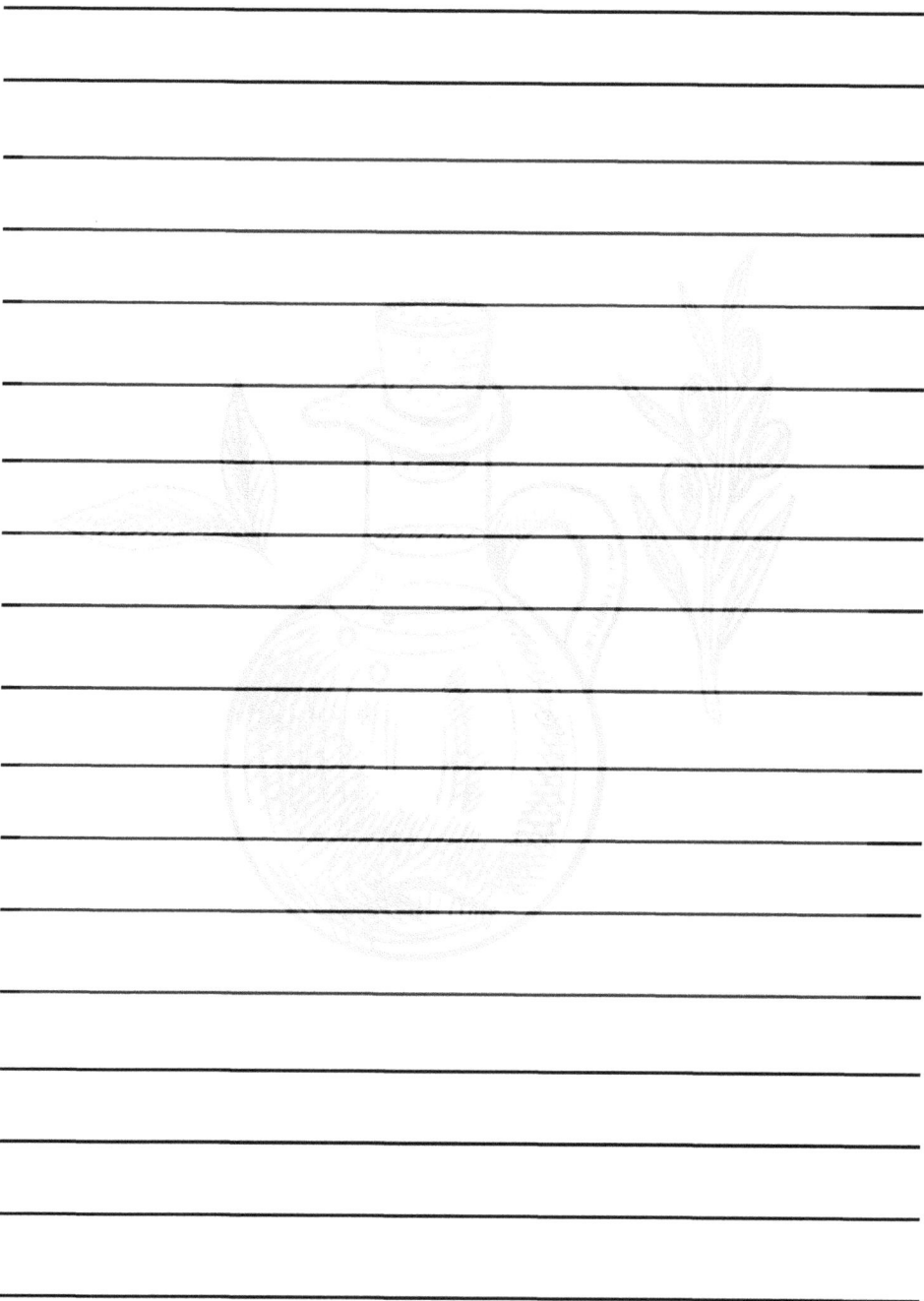

Day 3

Exodus 39:37

the pure gold lampstand with its row of lamps and all its accessories, and the olive oil for the light;

Exodus 25:6

  olive oil for the light; spices for the anointing oil and for the fragrant incense;

MEDITATION

The oil is light that illuminates how we live and move.

Take a moment to think about, write down and celebrate the light of the oil in your life.

Where in your life or heart do you need to make room for the oil to shine?

Cinnamon

SPIRITUAL MEANING: Holy anointing oil, attracts wealth and prosperity.

ORIGIN:

Cinnamon oil is obtained by the steam distillation of leaves from plants in the Cinnamomum Verum Tree and Cinnamomum Cassia Tree.

BENEFITS:

Antibacterial, antifungal, antioxidant properties, reduce (flatulence) gas, stimulates appetite, and aids in the increase of blood flow.

BLENDS WITH:

Ginger, Frankincense, Bergamot, Lavender, Lemon, Wild Orange, Ylang Ylang, Peppermint and Rosemary.

DIFFUSER BLENDS:

Fire and Ice
5 drops Peppermint
3 drops Cinnamon
4 drops Rosemary

Study Blend
4 drops Cinnamon
3 drops Peppermint

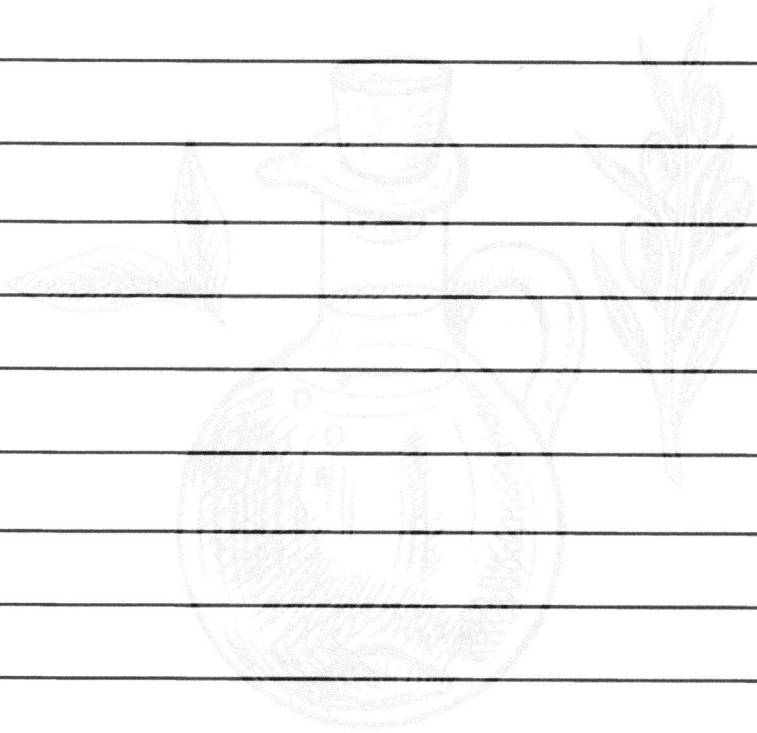

Day 4

SCRIPTURE

1 Samuel 16: 10-13

10 Jesse had seven of his sons pass before Samuel, but Samuel said to him, "The LORD has not chosen these." 11 So he asked Jesse, "Are these all the sons you have?"
"There is still the youngest," Jesse answered. "He is tending the sheep."
Samuel said, "Send for him; we will not sit down until he arrives."
12 So he sent for him and had him brought in. He was glowing with health and had a fine appearance and handsome features.
Then the LORD said, "Rise and anoint him; this is the one."
13 So Samuel took the horn of oil and anointed him in the presence of his brothers, and from that day on the Spirit of the LORD came powerfully upon David. Samuel then went to Ramah.

MEDITATION:
Just as a shepherd boy was anointed to become king of Israel, the oil supernaturally qualifies you for positions you are not equipped for in the natural.

Write about a time you saw the oil supernaturally move in your life. Remind yourself of how good it felt.

What do you want the oil to supernaturally qualify you for?

Clary Sage

SPIRITUAL MEANING: Wisdom of sages (get in touch with our creative self and dream work).

ORIGIN:

Clary Sage oil derives from a stout biennial herb, and is extracted through a process of steam distillation using the flowering tip and leaves. The plant is a native of Southern Europe.

BENEFITS:

Used to alleviate stress, sooth irritated skin, promote confidence & positivity, and relieve menopausal symptoms and cramps.

BLENDS WITH:

Lavender, Frankincense, Lemongrass, Cedarwood, and Patchouli.

DIFFUSER BLENDS:

Peaceful Rest
3 drops Clary Sage
2 drops Lavender
2 drops Cedarwood

Floral Peace
3 drops Clary Sage
3 drops Lavender
3 drops Patchouli

Day 5

SCRIPTURE

Psalm 133:2
It is like precious oil poured on the head,
 running down on the beard,
running down on Aaron's beard,
down on the collar of his robe.

MEDITATION

Oil is thick and runs slow. What was Aaron doing while the oil was running down his beard to the collar of his robe?   He was being still in his worship and letting the oil flow.

In what ways can you practice stillness so the oil in your life can flow?

Clove Bud

SPIRITUAL MEANING: Builds confidence and increases inner courage.

ORIGIN:

Clove Bud essential oil comes from the dried buds of the Syzygium Aromaticum tree. Native to the Spiced Island of Indonesia. All parts of the clove tree contain essential oils. It is through the process of steam distillation that the oil is extracted.

BENEFITS:

Used for dental care and toothaches. Relieves muscle aches and pains. Aids in digestion and upset stomach. Used in healing bruises and cuts.

BLENDS WITH:

Bergamot, Cinnamon, Peppermint, Clary Sage, Eucalyptus, and Rosemary.

DIFFUSER BLENDS:

Winter Freshness
5 drops Peppermint
3 drops Cinnamon
3 drops Clove

Open Airways
4 drops Rosemary
3 drops Clove
3 drops Eucalyptus

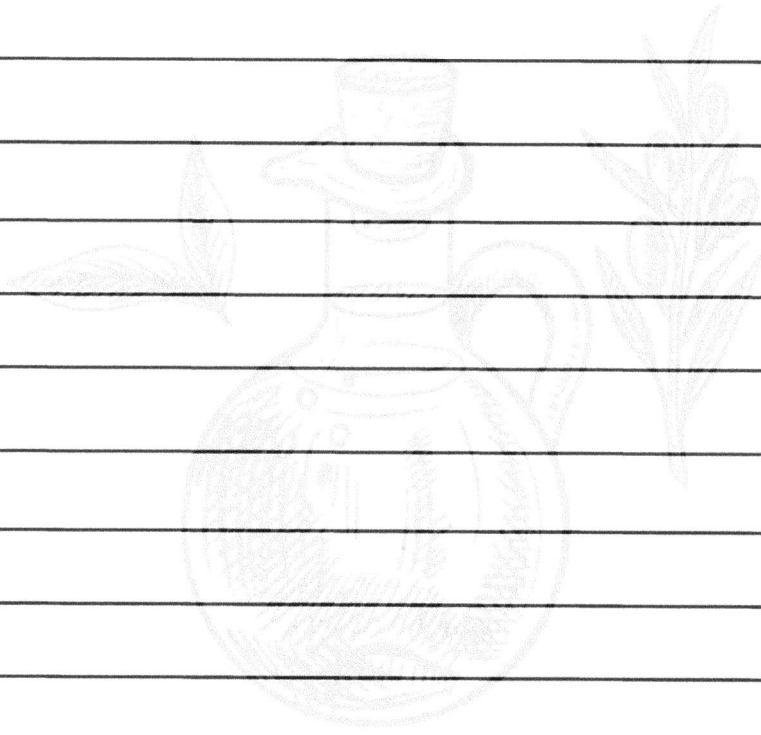

Day 6

SCRIPTURE

1 Samuel 10:1
Then Samuel took a flask of olive oil and poured it on Saul's head and kissed him, saying, "Has not the LORD anointed you ruler over his inheritance?

1 Samuel 16: 12 - 13
12 So he sent for him and had him brought in. He was glowing with health and had a fine appearance and handsome features.
Then the LORD said, "Rise and anoint him; this is the one."
13 So Samuel took the horn of oil and anointed him in the presence of his brothers, and from that day on the Spirit of the LORD came powerfully upon David. Samuel then went to Ramah.
14 Now the Spirit of the LORD had departed from Saul, and an evil spirit from the LORD tormented him.

MEDITATION

Samuel anointed both Saul and David. If you don't live, love, respect and move in your oil, it will be given to someone else, just as the oil anointing left Saul and was given to David.

Write down one area in our life that you know without any doubt your oil is absolutely flowing.

Think of a space in your life in which you are not moving fully in the oil. Write down one to three action steps you can take to press, so the oil can be released to flow.

Eucalyptus

SPIRITUAL MEANING: Healing and protection. Represents earth and heaven.

ORIGIN:

Eucalyptus essential oil comes from the leaves of the Eucalyptus tree species from the Myralaceae family native to Australia. The leaves are dried and crushed before undergoing steam distillation to produce the oil.

BENEFITS:

Used as relief of nasal congestion, common cold and even asthma. Helps with focus. Eases joint and muscle pain. Relieves insect bites. Fights dandruff and stimulates the scalp.

BLENDS WITH:

Lavender, Sandalwood, Peppermint, Lemon, and Rosemary.

DIFFUSER BLENDS:

Respiratory Rescue
3 drops Eucalyptus
3 drops Peppermint
2 drops Lemon
2 drops Rosemary

Tranquil Spa
3 drops Lavender
3 drops Eucalyptus
2 drops Sandalwood

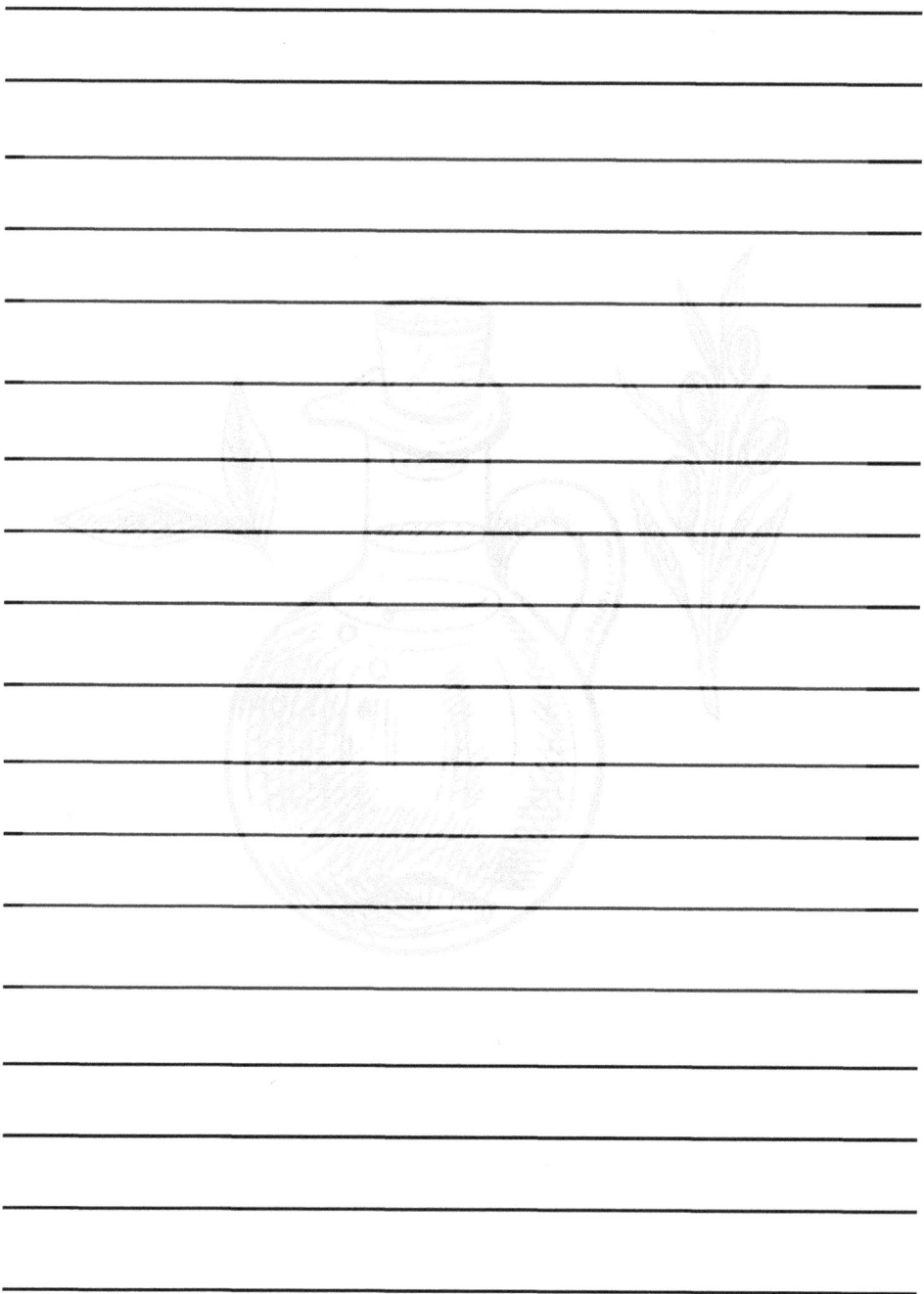

Day 7

The widow's oil - 2 Kings 4: 1-7

The wife of a man from the company of the prophets cried out to Elisha, "Your servant my husband is dead, and you know that he revered the LORD. But now his creditor is coming to take my two boys as his slaves."

2 Elisha replied to her, "How can I help you? Tell me, what do you have in your house?"

"Your servant has nothing there at all," she said, "except a small jar of olive oil."

3 Elisha said, "Go around and ask all your neighbors for empty jars. Don't ask for just a few. 4 Then go inside and shut the door behind you and your sons. Pour oil into all the jars, and as each is filled, put it to one side."

5 She left him and shut the door behind her and her sons. They brought the jars to her and she kept pouring. 6 When all the jars were full, she said to her son, "Bring me another one."

But he replied, "There is not a jar left." Then the oil stopped flowing.

7 She went and told the man of God, and he said, "Go, sell the oil and pay your debts. You and your sons can live on what is left."

MEDITATION

Each of us possess oil; at times where we lack is the press. The prophet told the widow to go inside and shut the door behind her. She had to quiet the noise and not focus on the external press of her sons potentially being taken away. She had some pressing of her own to do by pouring oil into the jars she had collected from her neighbors. Her press was private but her oil was public. She was able to pay the creditor, protect her sons, and have oil left over to live on.

Where do you need to do some private pressing?

Frankincense

SPIRITUAL MEANING: Divinity of Christ. The daddy of essential oils.

ORIGIN:

It originates from Africa, India & the Middle East from five species of Boswellia trees. It is extracted by steam distillation. Frankincense is called the King of the Oils and is frequently used in perfumes and incense.

BENEFITS:

May reduce arthritis. Improves gut function, asthma, oral health. Aids in reducing stress, anxiety and depression. Promotes smooth skin and balances hormones.

BLENDS WITH:

Cinnamon, Lavender, Lemon, Myrrh, Patchouli and Ylang Ylang, Peppermint and Cedarwood.

DIFFUSER BLENDS:

Morning Yoga
4 drops Frankincense
3 drops Peppermint
2 drops Lavender

Frankly Relaxing
4 drops Frankincense
3 drops Cedarwood
2 drops Lavender

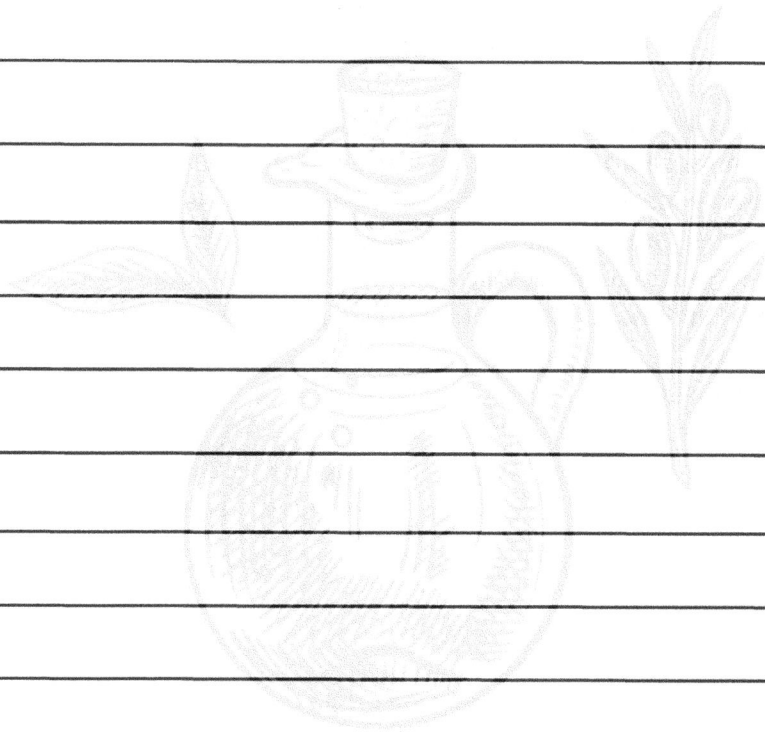

Day 8

2 Kings 9: 1- 6

The prophet Elisha summoned a man from the company of the prophets and said to him, "Tuck your cloak into your belt, take this flask of olive oil with you and go to Ramoth Gilead.
2 When you get there, look for Jehu son of Jehoshaphat, the son of Nimshi. Go to him, get him away from his companions and take him into an inner room.
3 Then take the flask and pour the oil on his head and declare, 'This is what the LORD says: I anoint you king over Israel.' Then open the door and run; don't delay!"
4 So the young prophet went to Ramoth Gilead.
5 When he arrived, he found the army officers sitting together. "I have a message for you, commander," he said.
"For which of us?" asked Jehu.
"For you, commander," he replied.
6 Jehu got up and went into the house. Then the prophet poured the oil on Jehu's head and declared, "This is what the LORD, the God of Israel, says: 'I anoint you king over the LORD's people Israel."

MEDITATION

The oil sets you apart for specific assignments. Don't fret when others can't go with you. Your assignment at times is a private matter between you and Yahweh.

What oil do you need to keep private for right now until the Lord instructs you to make it public?

Ginger

SPIRITUAL MEANING: Symbol of strength.

ORIGIN:

Ginger essential oil or Ginger Root is derived from the root of the Zingiber officinale herb from India. It comes from a tropical perennial herb and is steam distilled.

BENEFITS:

Used for upset stomach, digestive issues, nausea, respiratory problems. Aids in healing infections. Decreases inflammation, anxiety, headaches, and muscle pain.

BLENDS WITH:

Wild Orange, Clove, Eucalyptus, Frankincense & Peppermint and Lemon.

DIFFUSER BLENDS:

Zen Concentration
3 drops Frankincense
3 drops Wild Orange
3 drops Ginger

Better Breathing
2 drops Peppermint
2 drops Eucalyptus
2 drops Lemon
2 drops Ginger

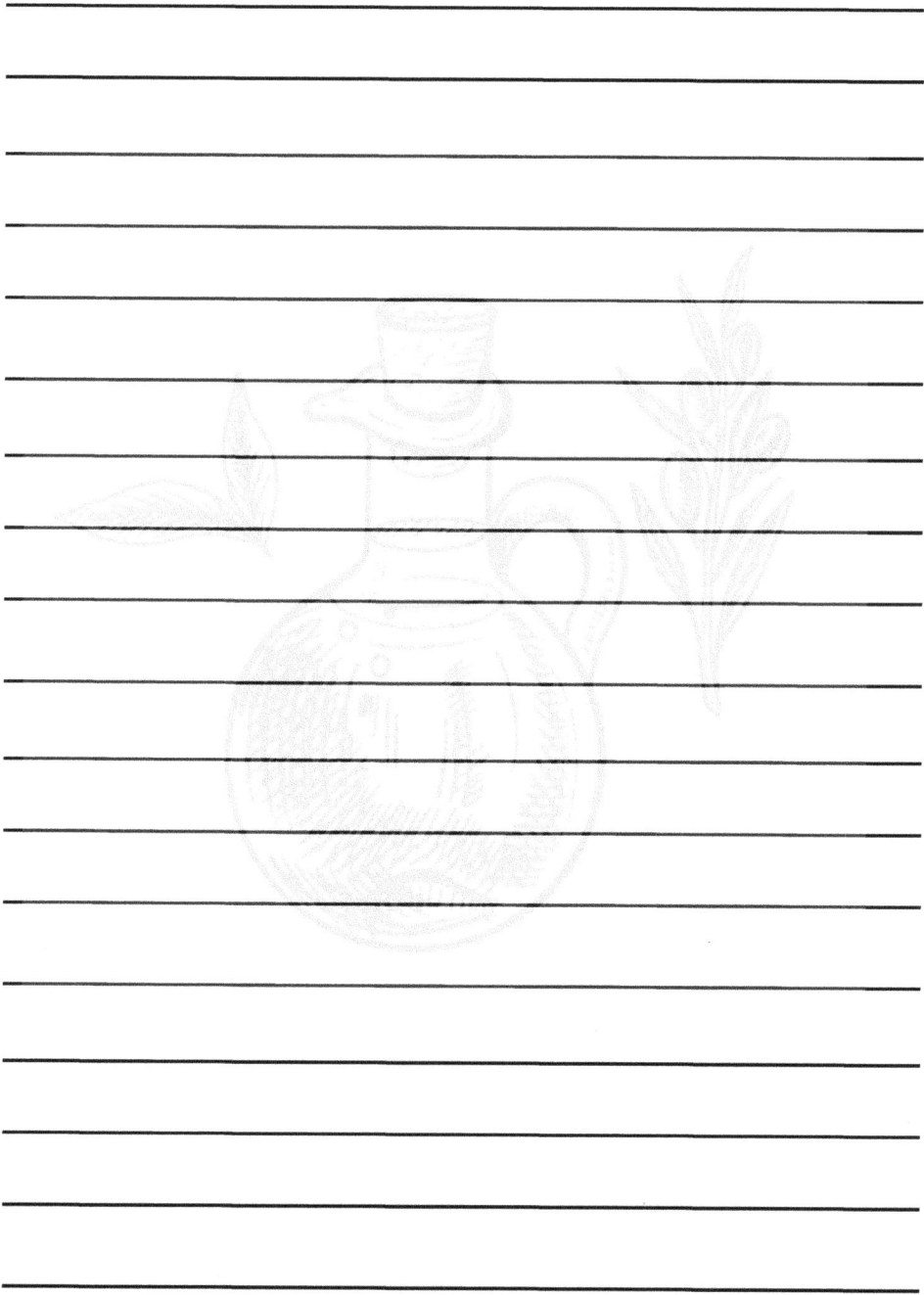

Day 9

SCRIPTURE

Psalm 92:10
You have exalted my horn like that of a wild ox;
   fine oils have been poured on me.

MEDITATION

Know without any doubt you are blessed and anointed.

Take a moment and list some of the oil (blessings) in your life.

Herlichrysum

SPIRITUAL MEANING: Instills deep peace and tranquility. Aids in releasing emotional trauma.

ORIGIN:
Helichrysum oil comes from the Helichrysum italicum plant, which is generally found in the Mediterranean and Southern Europe. The common method of obtaining the oil is by steam distilling the tips and stems of fresh helichrysum flowers.

BENEFITS:

Relieves allergies. Can be used to stop bleeding and aid wound healing. Reduces inflammation of the muscles and joints, bloating, insomnia, indigestion, and acid reflux.

BLENDS WITH:

Clary Sage, Lavender, Wild Orange, Frankincense, Sandalwood, Bergamot, Lemon, Eucalyptus and Peppermint.

DIFFUSER BLENDS:

Evening Relaxation
4 drops Lavender
4 drops Bergamot
2 drops Lemon
2 drops Helichrysum

Fresh Linen
2 drops Lavender
3 drops Eucalyptus
2 drops Lemon
1 drop Peppermint
2 drops Helichrysum

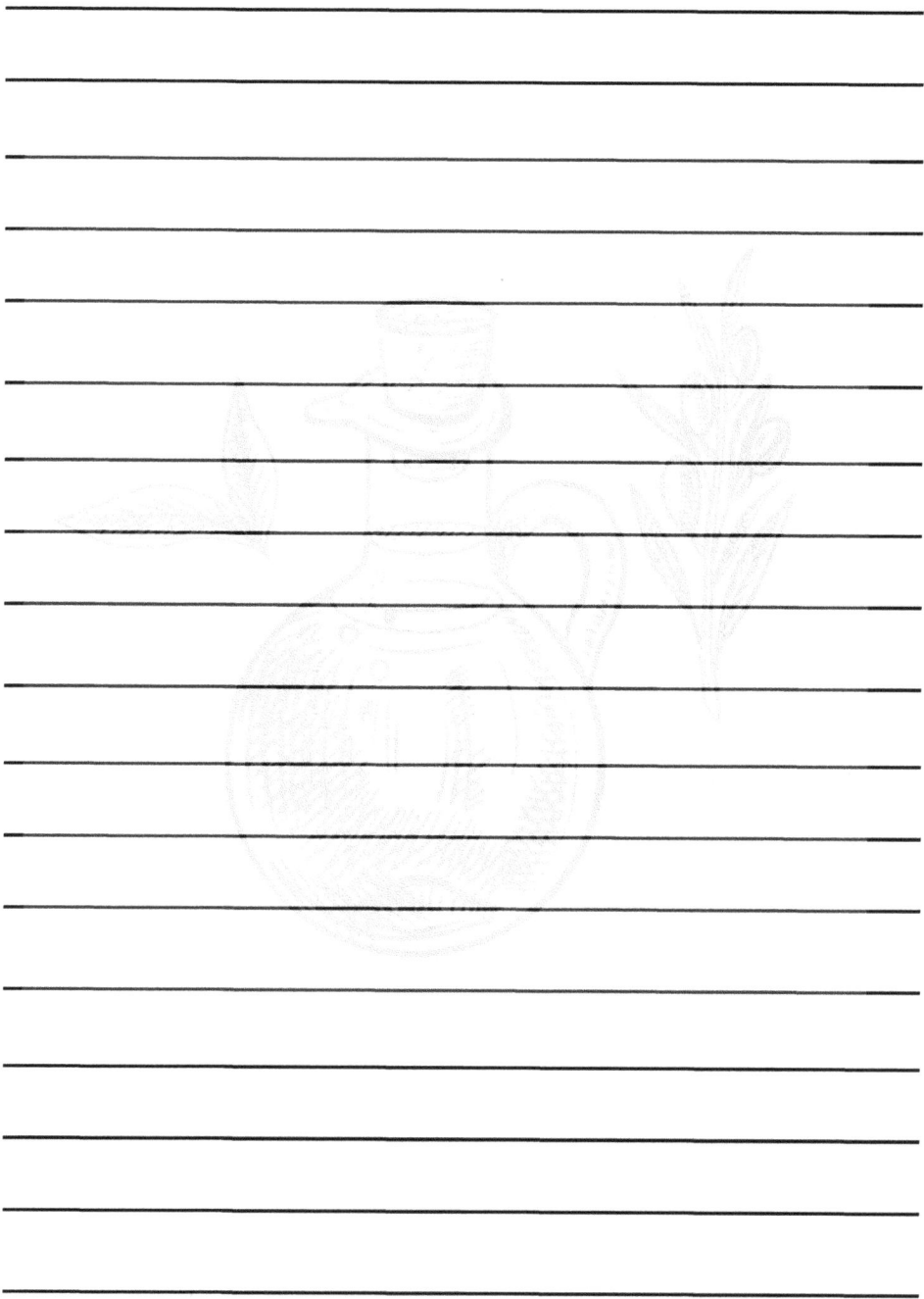

Day 10

Psalm 104:15
wine that gladdens human hearts,
   oil to make their faces shine,
   and bread that sustains their hearts.

MEDITATION

The Oil of the Holy Spirit gives you a glow.

What's glowing in your life right now?

In what areas of your life would you like to see more of the oil's shine?

Lavender

SPIRITUAL MEANING: Purification rituals; healing.

ORIGIN:

Lavender essential oil is obtained by steam distillation of certain Lavender species. Lavender is found in Bulgaria, Spain, and France.

BENEFITS:

Add to relaxation. Relieves burns, insect bites. Reduces stress and anxiety. Reduces wrinkles, acne, and pain. Can be used in hair care for disinfecting the scalp and boosting hair growth.

BLENDS WITH:

Wild Orange, Cedarwood, Ylang Ylang, Clary Sage, Ginger, Cinnamon, Bergamot and Frankincense.

DIFFUSER BLENDS:

Dream Weaver
4 drops Lavender
2 drops Wild Orange
2 drops Cedarwood
1 drop Ylang Ylang

Time to Pause
3 drops Lavender
2 drops Clary Sage
2 drops Ginger
1 drop Cinnamon

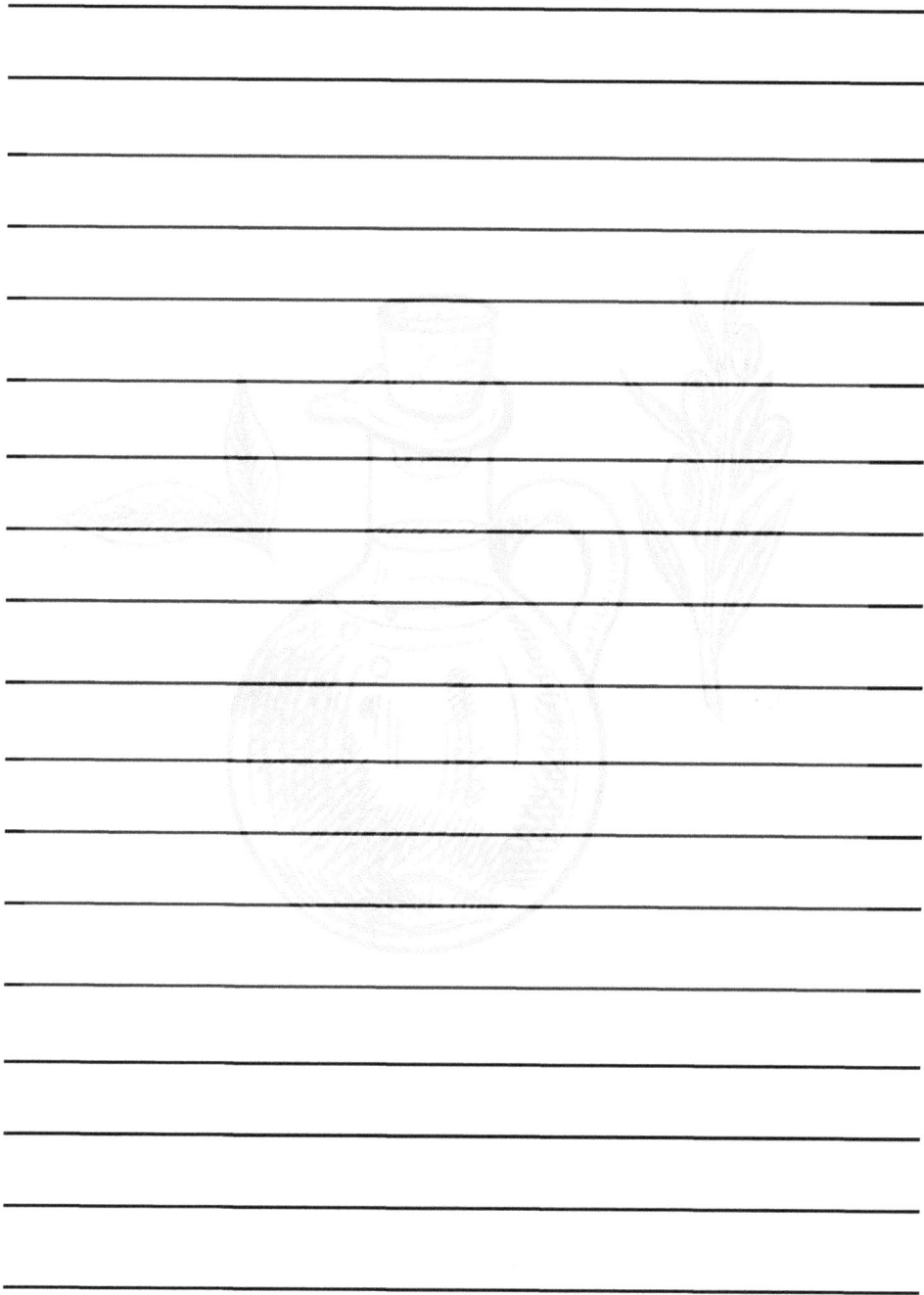

Day 11

Psalm 23:5
You prepare a table before me
   in the presence of my enemies.
You anoint my head with oil;
   my cup overflows.

MEDITATION

The oil expands us.

Take a moment to journal about how the oil has expanded you.

Where in your life or heart would you like to experience more of the oil's expansion power?

Lemon

SPIRITUAL MEANING: Hope, fertility, perfection and abundance.

ORIGIN:

Lemon essential oil is extracted from the lemon rinds or peel of the lemon. A cold press distillation process is typically used for producing oils from citrus plants.

BENEFITS:

Moisturizes and smooths dry skin. Enhances metabolism, reduces gas, purifies the air and surfaces. Energizes the mind and body. Aids in weight control and digestion. Adds in heart health.

BLENDS WITH:

Lavender, Bergamot, Peppermint, Wild Orange, Frankincense, and Rosemary.

DIFFUSER BLENDS:

Allergy Blends
2 drops Lemon
2 drops Peppermint
2 drops Lavender

Energizer Bunny
2 drops Lavender
2 drops Wild Orange
2 drops Rosemary
2 drops Lemon

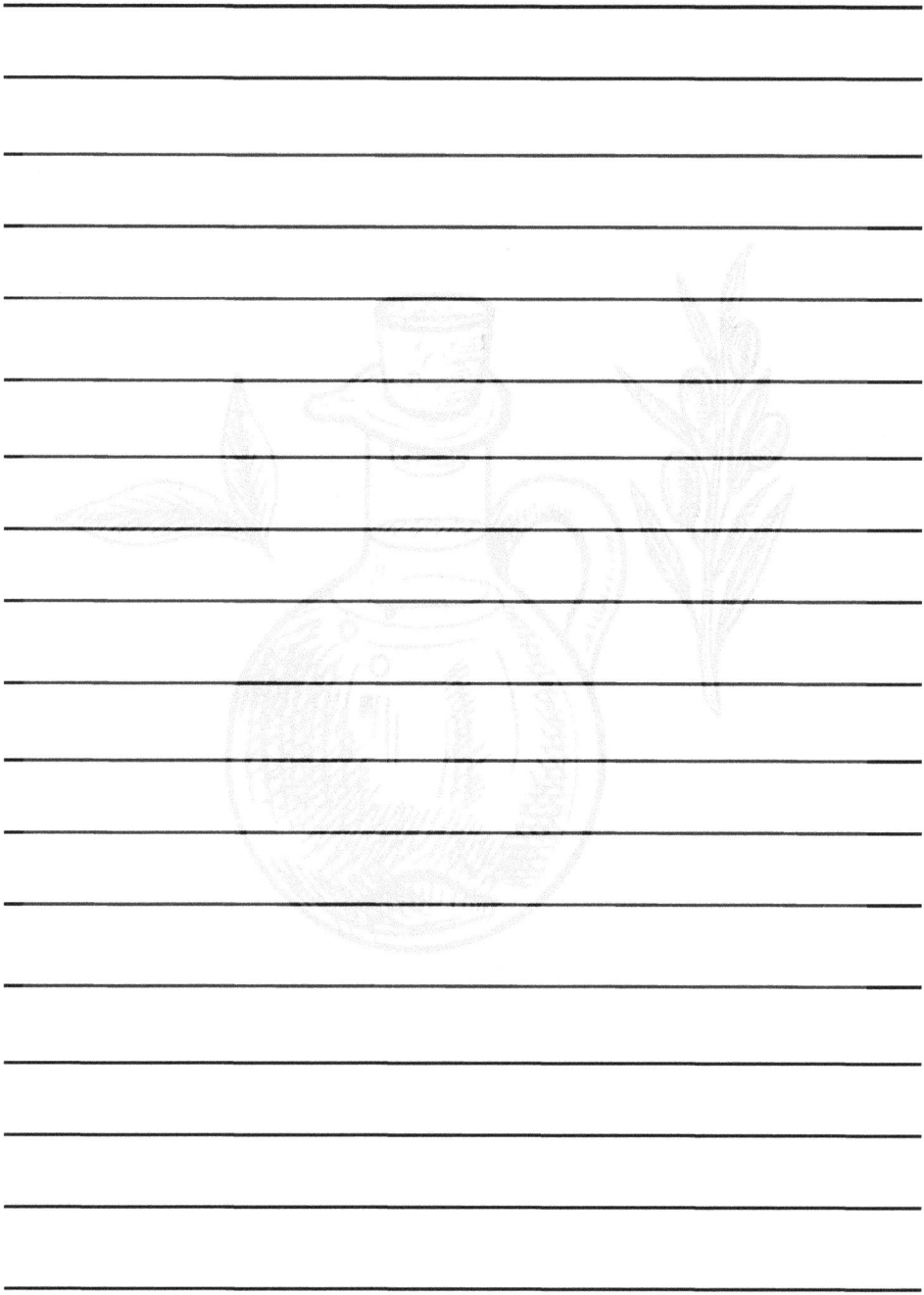

Day 12

1 John 2:27
As for you, the anointing you received from him remains in you, and you do not need anyone to teach you. But as his anointing teaches you about all things and as that anointing is real, not counterfeit—just as it has taught you, remain in him.

MEDITATION

The oil of the Holy Spirit gives us wisdom.

We know a lot of things in this day and age. But do we always apply what we know? Wisdom is applied knowledge.

 Are there any areas in your life where you desire to have the oil drip on something you know, so it can be applied and become wisdom?

Lemongrass

SPIRITUAL MEANING: (Calamus) Used as anointing oil applied to priests of the tabernacle.

ORIGIN:

Lemongrass essential oil has its origins in Southeast Asia, although it is now cultivated in countries around the world. It is distilled from the leaves and woody stalks of the lemongrass plant and produces a subtle citrus-herb scent. It is derived from steam distillation of the fresh or partly dried lemongrass leaves.

BENEFITS:

Reduces inflammation, relieves muscle aches and body pains including headaches and discomforts associated with arthritis. Used as a toner and antiseptic.

BLENDS WITH:

Cedarwood, Sandalwood, Lavender, Lemon, Helichrysum, and Eucalyptus

DIFFUSER BLENDS:

Breath of Fresh Air
3 drops Lemongrass
3 drops Lavender
3 drops Eucalyptus

Meditation
4 drops Lemongrass
4 drops Sandalwood

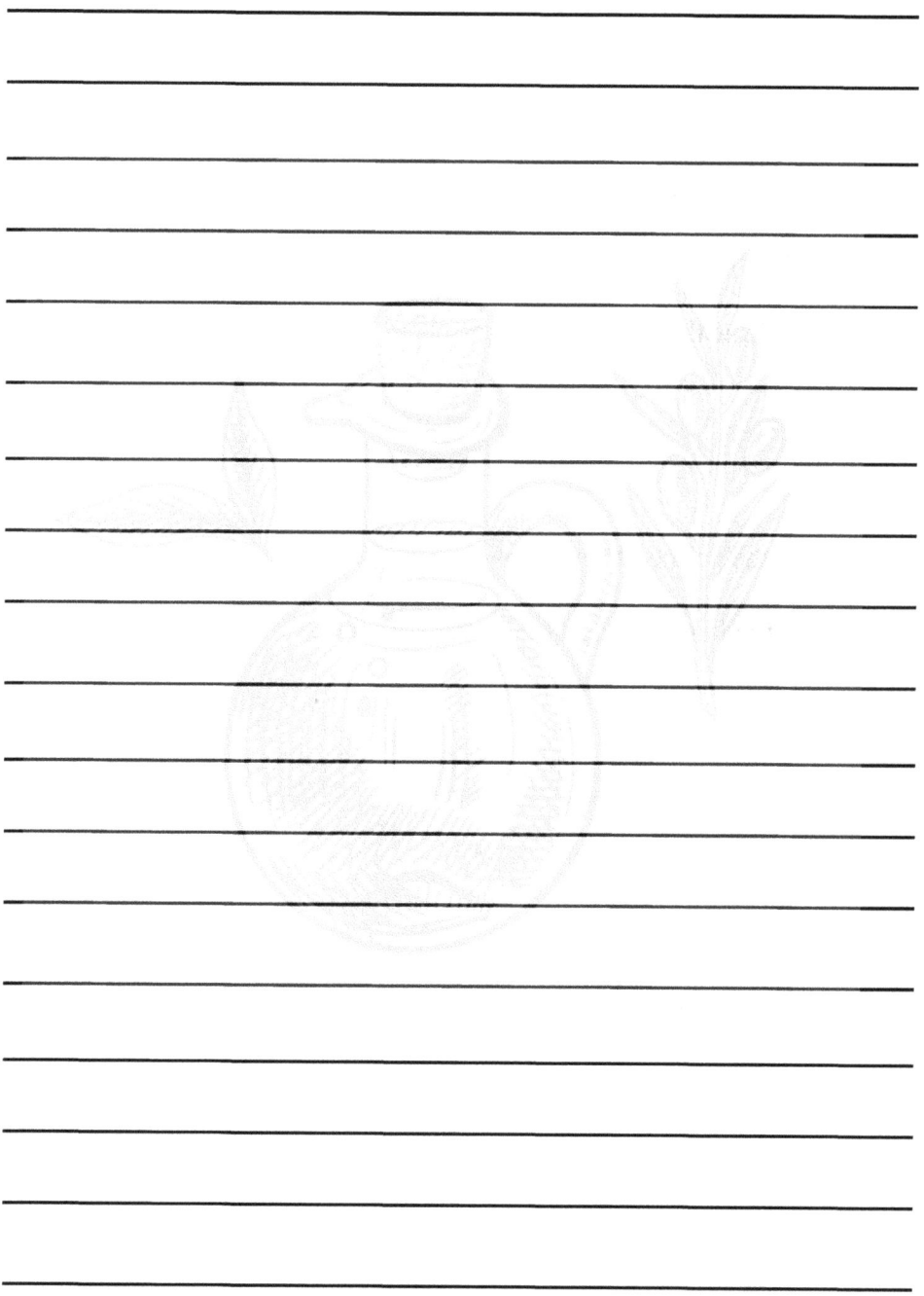

Day 13

SCRIPTURE

Esther 2:12 Before a young woman's turn came to go into King Xerxes, she had to complete twelve months of beauty treatments prescribed for the women, six months with oil of myrrh and six with perfumes and cosmetics.

MEDITATION

The oil prepares us.

Before Esther entered the palace, she had no idea what she was being prepared for.

Write a prayer asking the Lord to send HIS oil to prepare you for the unknown.

Myrrh

SPIRITUAL MEANING: An anointing oil used as gifts to Kings. Represents Holiness.

ORIGIN:

Myrrh essential oil is a gum-resin extracted from several small thorny tree species of the genus commiphora. A tree commonly used in the production of Myrrh can be found in the shallow rocky soils of Ethiopia. Myrrh resin has been used throughout history as a perfume, incense, and medicine. The oil is produced by steam distillation.

BENEFITS:

Antibacterial, anti-fungal, anti-inflammatory, and beneficial for the overall health of your stomach. Relieves excess mucus and phlegm. Aids in reducing congestion, breathing trouble and heaviness in the chest. Great against acne and wrinkles. Eases anxiety.

BLENDS WITH:

Frankincense, Lavender, Eucalyptus, Lemon, Wild Orange, Clove, Patchouli, and Sandalwood.

DIFFUSER BLENDS:

Uplift
2 drops Myrrh
2 drops Frankincense
2 drops Lemon

Peaceful Evening
2 drops Myrrh
2 drops Sandalwood
3 drops Lavender

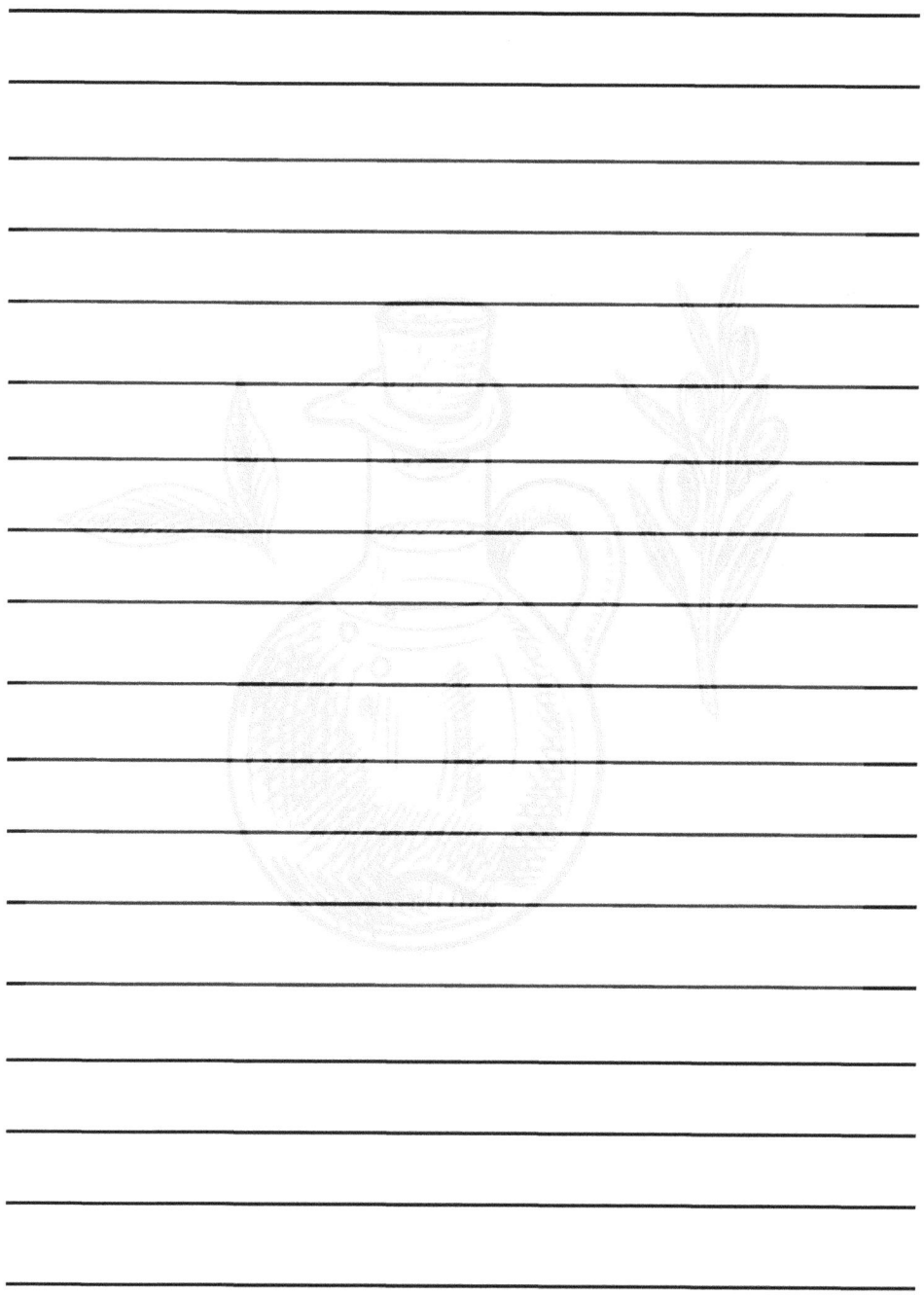

Day 14

James 5:14
 Is anyone among you sick? Let them call the elders of the church to pray over them and anoint them with oil in the name of the Lord.

MEDITATION

The oil of the Lord has the power to heal us physically, mentally and spiritually.

Thank the Lord for the spaces in your life that the oil has healed.

Where are you still in need of the oil's healing power?

Oregano

SPIRITUAL MEANING: Love and Romance. Good health.

ORIGIN:

Oregano essential oil comes from the popular oregano plant, which is a member of the mint family and is native to areas of western Asia and the Mediterranean. Oregano essential oil is steam distilled as the extraction process. Oregano odor is pungent, and its flowers are quite colorful.

BENEFITS:

Strengthens the immune system. Aids as an antibacterial. Reduces congestion. Pain relief, antifungal, cleansing, digestion and purifying.

BLENDS WITH:

Lemon, Wild Orange, Frankincense, Peppermint, Lavender, Rosemary, Bergamot, Cedarwood.

DIFFUSER BLEND:

Clean the Air
1 drop Oregano
4 drops Lemon
3 drops Wild Orange

Blocked Nose
1 drop Oregano
4 drops Lemon
3 drops Peppermint

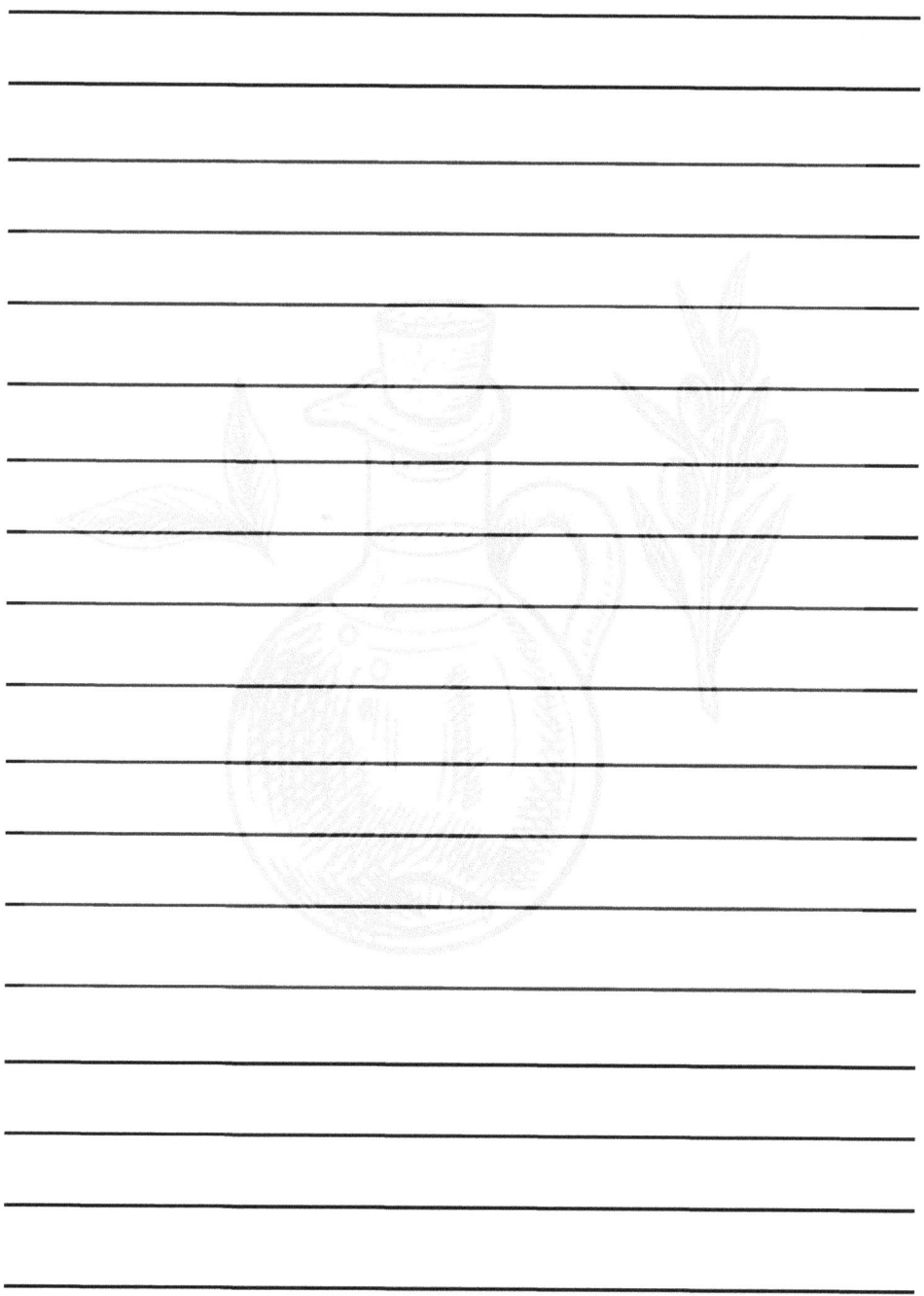

Day 15

SCRIPTURE

Matthew 6:17
But when you fast, put oil on your head and wash your face.

MEDITATION

The oil sustains us.

Celebrate and write about a time the oil sustained you during your press.

Patchouli

SPIRITUAL MEANING: Love and fertility. Aphrodisiac.

ORIGIN:

Patchouli essential oil comes from Indonesia. It is steam distilled from the large furry leaves to produce a thick dark oil, yellowish brown in color.

BENEFITS:

Used as a calming agent and skin tonic. Fights against wrinkles, fungal infections, insect bites and heals open sores and wounds. Relieves sunburn.

BLENDS WITH:

Sandalwood, Bergamot, Cedarwood, Wild Orange, Lavender, Myrrh, Lemongrass, Clary Sage, Ylang Ylang, Frankincense and Clove.

DIFFUSER BLENDS:

Courage Blends
4 drops Patchouli
2 drops Clove
2 drops Sandalwood

Lavender Patchouli Bath Blend
4 drops Lavender
2 drops Patchouli
1 tablespoon Castile Soap
Mix essential oils into Castile Soap, add to warm bath

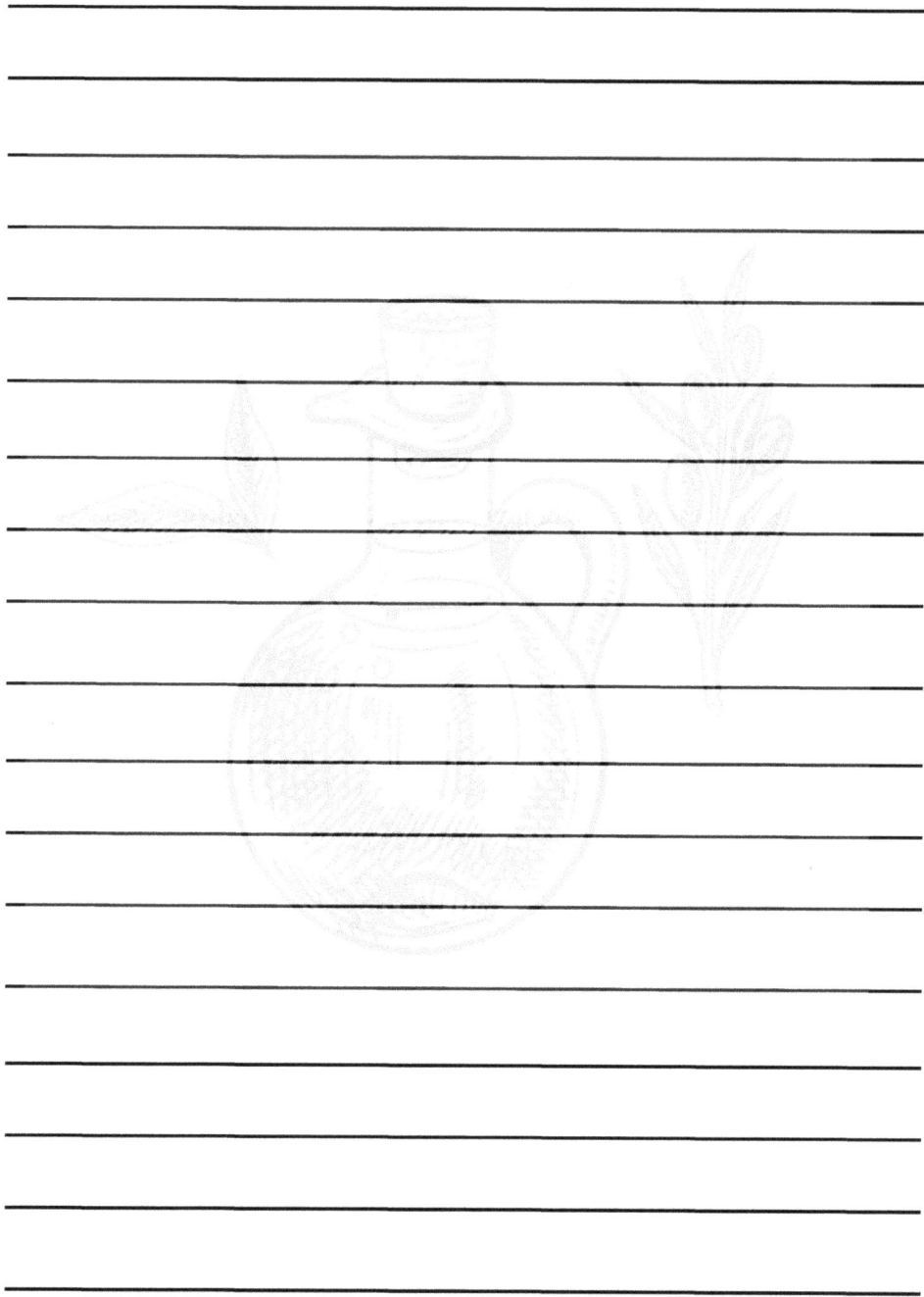

Day 16

SCRIPTURE

Leviticus 10:7
Do not leave the entrance to the tent of meeting or you will die, because the LORD's anointing oil is on you." So they did as Moses said.

MEDITATION

The Oil of the Lord protects us from dangers seen and unseen.

Write the Lord a thank you note for the oil's protection over you and your loved ones.

Peppermint

SPIRITUAL MEANING: Cleanse, money, energy.

ORIGIN:

Peppermint (Mentha piperita) is an aromatic perennial plant that grows to a height of about three feet. It has light purple flowers and green leaves. Peppermint grows throughout North America, Asia, and Europe. Peppermint is steam distilled using the entire herb.

BENEFITS:

Relieves muscle and joint pain. Aids in sinus and respiratory issues as well as seasonal allergy relief. Increases energy and improves exercises performance. A digestive aid for upset stomachs. Helps to relieve hot flashes and good for headaches.

BLENDS WELL:

Lavender, Lemon, Wild Orange, Eucalyptus, Cedarwood, Rosemary, Frankincense

DIFFUSER BLENDS:

Energizing Blend
4 drops Peppermint
5 drops Wild Orange

Breath Easy
3 drops Eucalyptus
3 drops Peppermint
3 drops Rosemary

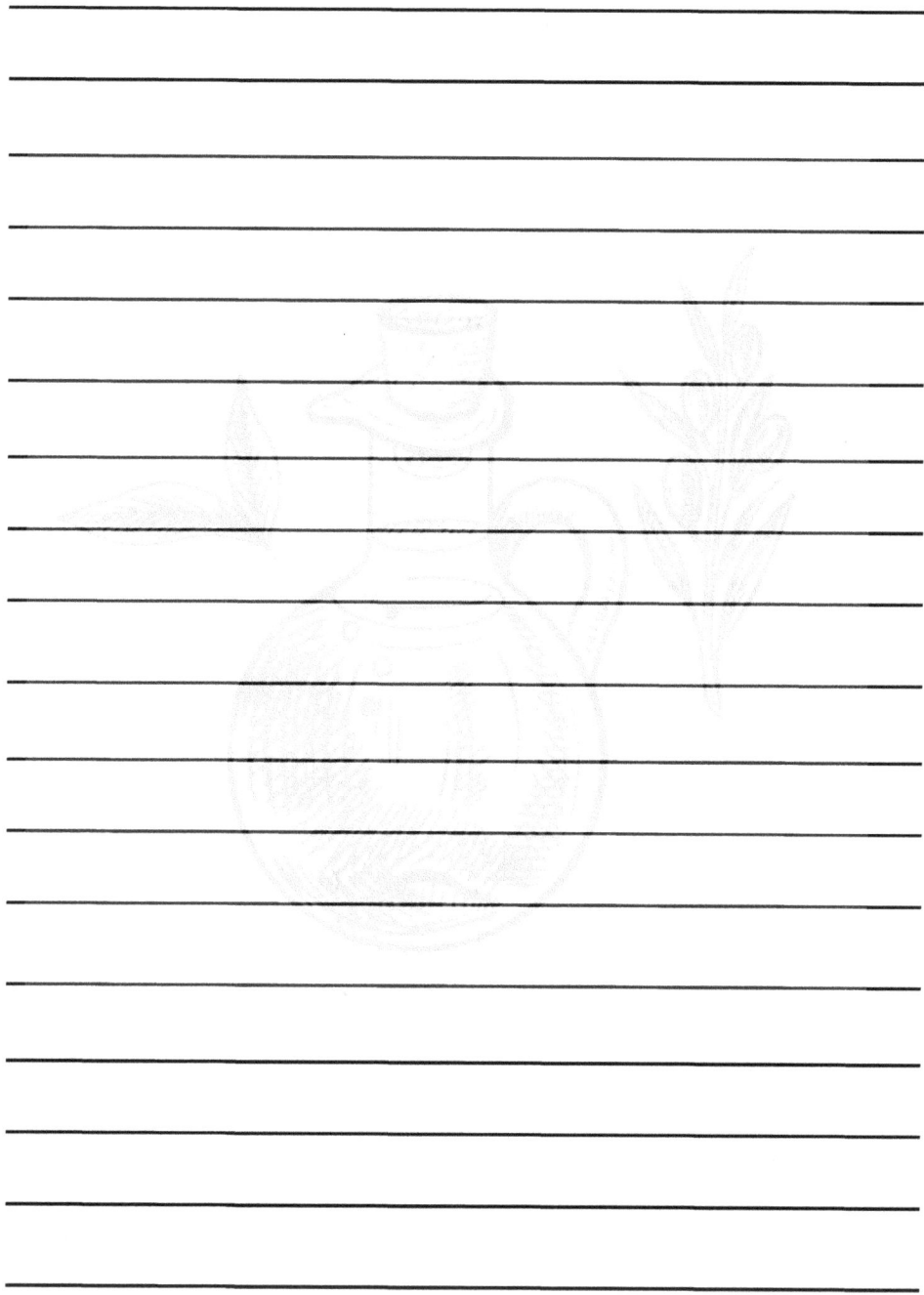

Day 17

Psalm 45:7
You love righteousness and hate wickedness;
  therefore God, your God, has set you above your companions
  by anointing you with the oil of joy.

MEDITATION

The Oil of the Holy Spirit gives you joy.

Write out a list of things in your life that bring you joy.

Rosemary

SPIRITUAL MEANING: Dew of the sea. Signifies love and remembrance.

ORIGIN:

Rosemary is a perennial herb and a member of the mint family. It is incredibly fragrant with needle-like leaves and flowers that may be white, pink, blue or purple. This herb is native to the Mediterranean and is steam distilled to make Rosemary essential oil.

BENEFITS:

Can be used as an anti-inflammatory. Memory and concentration enhancer. Improves digestion. Used as an antioxidant. Stimulates hair growth. Repels certain bugs. May help relieve pain.

BLENDS WITH:

Lavender, Cedarwood, Frankincense, Lemongrass, Peppermint, Wild Orange, Lemon, Eucalyptus and Bergamot.

DIFFUSER BLENDS:

Spring Do
5 drops Lemon
2 drops Eucalyptus
2 drops Rosemary

Coastal Waters
1 drop Rosemary
1 drop Eucalyptus
2 drops Lemon
2 drops Bergamot

Creativity
1 drop Rosemary
1 drop Peppermint
2 drops Lemon
2 drops Frankincense

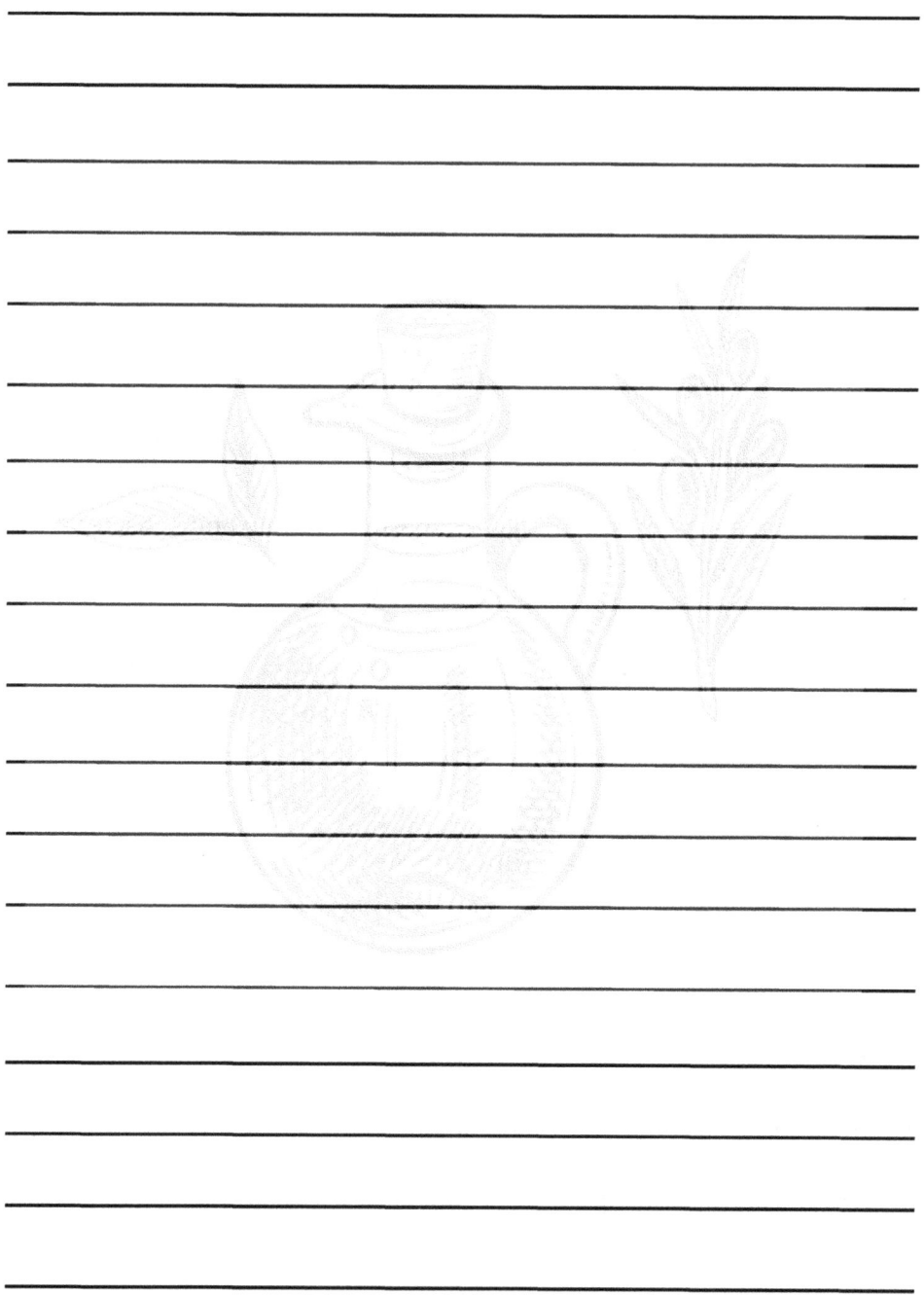

Day 18

Matthew 26:6-13
6 While Jesus was in Bethany in the home of Simon the Leper, 7 a woman came to him with an alabaster jar of very expensive perfume, which she poured on his head as he was reclining at the table.
8 When the disciples saw this, they were indignant. "Why this waste?" they asked. 9 "This perfume could have been sold at a high price and the money given to the poor." 10 Aware of this, Jesus said to them, "Why are you bothering this woman? She has done a beautiful thing to me. 11 The poor you will always have with you,[a] but you will not always have me. 12 When she poured this perfume on my body, she did it to prepare me for burial. 13 Truly I tell you, wherever this gospel is preached throughout the world, what she has done will also be told, in memory of her."
Mark 14:3
3 While he was in Bethany, reclining at the table in the home of Simon the Leper, a woman came with an alabaster jar of very expensive perfume, made of pure nard. She broke the jar and poured the perfume on his head.

John 12:3 Then Mary took about a pint of pure nard, an expensive perfume; she poured it on Jesus' feet and wiped his feet with her hair. And the house was filled with the fragrance of the perfume.

MEDITATION

The nard mentioned in the above passages is the oil Spikenard.

What does honoring the Lord with your oil look like?

What's your favorite form of worship? Singing, dancing, prayer, journaling or something else?

Spikenard

SPIRITUAL MEANING:

Inspires devotion. Aids in creating inner peace.

ORIGIN:

Spikenard, a flowering plant of the Valerian family, is native to high altitudes in the sub-alpine regions of the Himalayan Mountains. Spikenard essential oil is steam distilled from the roots of the plant and has been valued for centuries. It is traditionally used to anoint people of high honor.

BENEFITS:

Antibacterial and antifungal. Eases inflammation. Soothes the mind and body. Can be used as a laxative agent. Helps promote the health of reproductive organs. Boosts the immune system. Powerful deodorant for the home. Lowers blood pressure.

BLENDS WITH:

Clove, Frankincense, Lavender, Wild Orange, Patchouli, Lemon, and Peppermint.

RECIPES:

Add 2-4 drops of oil to a tub of warm bathing water for a calming and relaxing bath to soothe your mind.
To lower blood pressure or treat heart palpitations, you can gently rub a few drops of diluted Spikenard oil onto your feet or add it into a small tub to make a warm foot bath.

DIFFUSER BLENDS:

Brain Boost
2 drops Clove
2 drops Frankincense
1 drop Peppermint
2 drops Spikenard

Fresh Start
2 drops Spikenard
2 drops Lemon
3 drops Patchouli

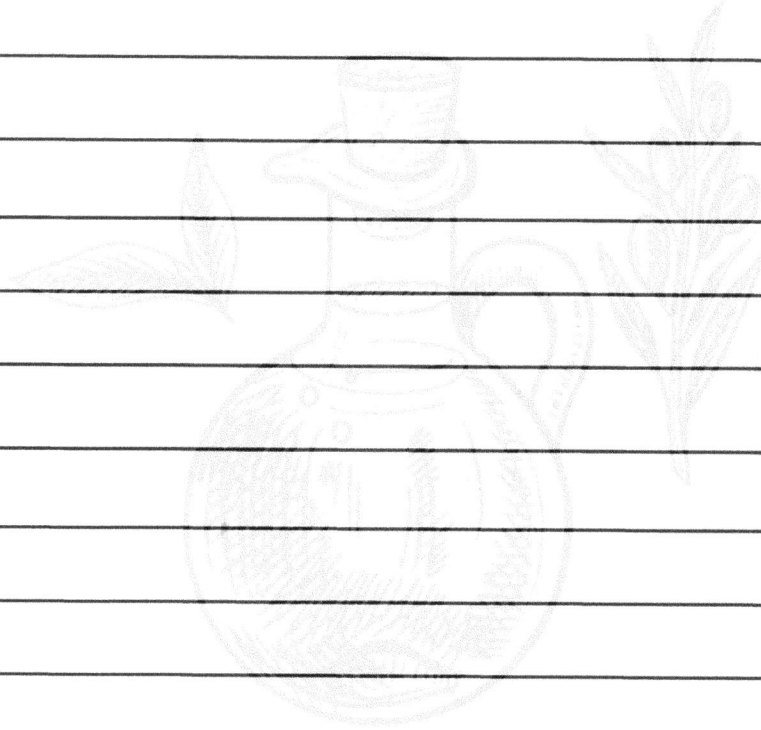

Day 19

Hosea 2: 8
She has not acknowledged that I was the one
    who gave her the grain, the new wine and oil,
who lavished on her the silver and gold—
    which they used for Baal.

MEDITATION

Do not squander your oil.

The Lord gives us spiritual oil through the Holy Spirit and physical oil from the earth through plants. In either form, be mindful of where your oil comes from.

In what ways have you squandered your oil and recognized your need for change?

Turmeric

SPIRITUAL MEANING: Purification.

ORIGIN:

Turmeric essential oil is derived from the plant tuberous rhizomes, or underground roots. The oil is typically obtained from turmeric root through steam distillation. Turmeric is sourced from various parts of India and Nepal.

BENEFITS:

Can be used as an antiseptic and controls acne. Promotes hair and scalp health. Prevents dandruff and dryness. Relieves stress, inflammation, and pain.

BLENDS WITH:

Lavender, Lemon, Peppermint, Wild Orange and Ginger

RECIPES:

Inflammation & Pain Relief
5 drops Turmeric
5 drops carrier oil (Jojoba or Coconut oil)
Apply to areas of concern

DIFFUSER BLENDS:

Stress Relief
2-3 drops Turmeric

All Seasons
2 drops Lavender
2 drops Lemon
2 drops Peppermint
2 drops Turmeric

Day 20

1 Kings 17: 12-16

12 "As surely as the Lord your God lives," she replied, "I don't have any bread–only a handful of flour in a jar and a little olive oil in a jug. I am gathering a few sticks to take home and make a meal for myself and my son, that we may eat it–and die." 13 Elijah said to her, 'Don't be afraid. Go home and do as you have said. But first make a small loaf of bread for me from what you have and bring it to me, and then make something for yourself and your son. 14 For this is what the Lord, the God of Israel, says; "The jar of flour will not be used up and the jug of oil will not run dry until the day the Lord sends rain on the land."'
15 She went away and did as Elijah had told her. So there was food every day for Elijah and for the woman and her family. 16 For the jar of flour was not used up and the jug of oil did not run dry, in keeping with the word of the Lord spoken by Elijah.

The widow of Zarephath definitely felt a press to share with the prophet out of the little bit she had.   She was clearly already feeling a press of desperation when she declared that she and her son were going to eat their last meal and die. But because she pressed in on the words of the prophet "The jar of flour will not be used up and the jug of oil will not run dry until the day the Lord sends rain on the land", and believed what he said, she was blessed.
The press is simply that - a pressing.

MEDITATION

Write a simple prayer asking the Father to give you the oil to believe in the press. The press produces the oil.

Wild Orange

SPIRITUAL MEANING: Abundance, richness, fertility, longevity, beauty.

ORIGIN:

Orange oil is extracted from the rind of the sweet orange. This is done by a method called cold pressing, which uses pressure to squeeze the oils from the rind. Sweet oranges are sourced from Greece and Brazil. Their climate and growing conditions contribute to the best possible orange citrus.

BENEFITS:

Lifts your mood, reduces stress, relieves upset stomach. Great household cleaner. Reduces pain and inflammation. Treats skin conditions such as acne.

BLENDS WELL WITH:

Lavender, Cinnamon, Frankincense, Bergamot, Lemon, Peppermint

DIFFUSER BLENDS:

Lift My Mood	Need to Study	Wake Up!
3 drops Wild Orange	3 drops Wild Orange	4 drops Peppermint
3 drops Bergamot	3 drops Peppermint	4 drops Wild Orange
3 drops Lemon	3 drops Frankincense	

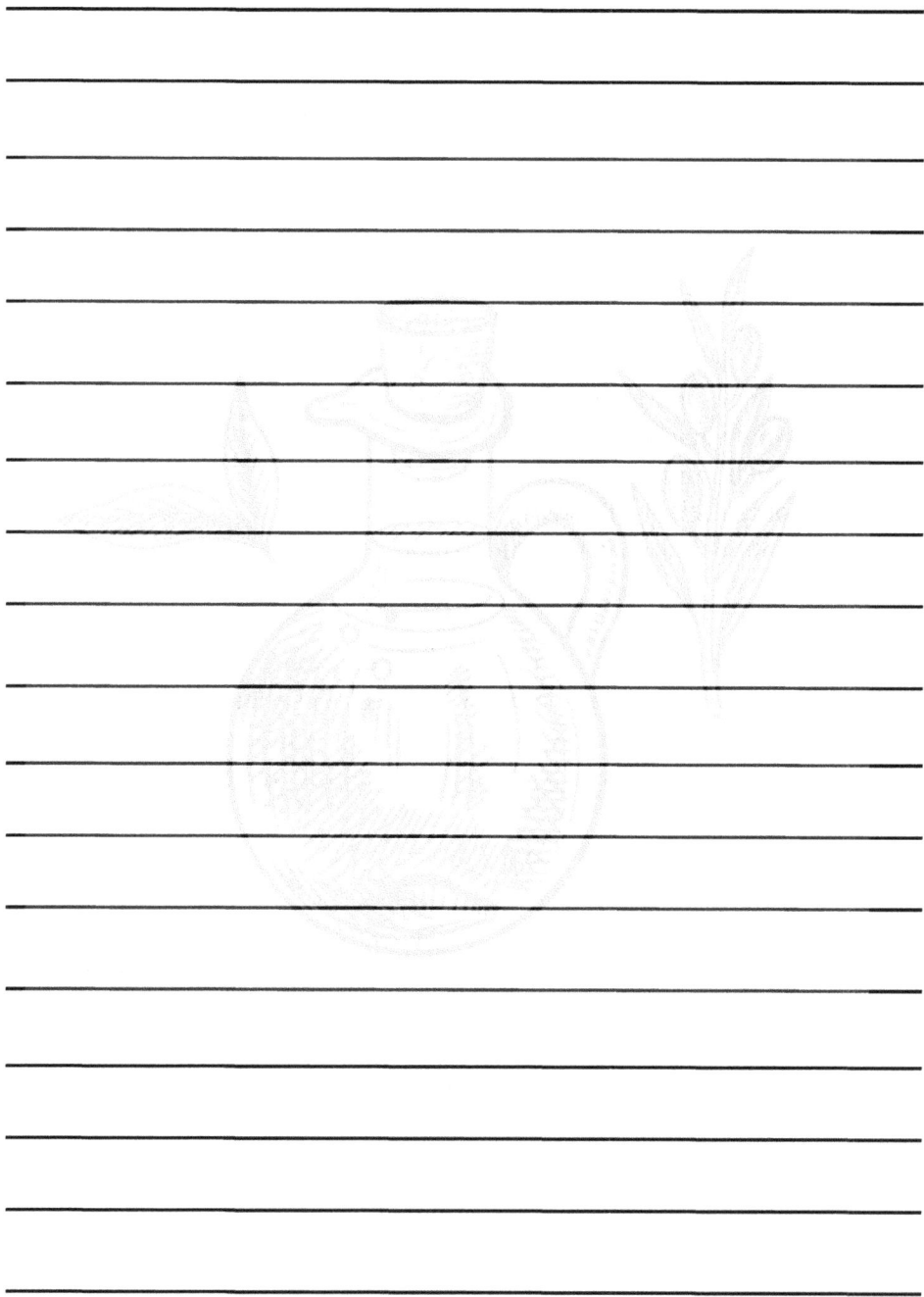

Day 21

Isaiah 52:13–15
See, my servant will act wisely;
   he will be raised and lifted up and highly exalted.
14 Just as there were many who were appalled at him[—
   his appearance was so disfigured beyond that of any human being
   and his form marred beyond human likeness—
15 so he will sprinkle many nations,
   and kings will shut their mouths because of him.
For what they were not told, they will see,
   and what they have not heard, they will understand.

Matthew 26:36-38
36 Then Jesus went with his disciples to a place called Gethsemane, and he said to them, "Sit here while I go over there and pray." 37 He took Peter and the two sons of Zebedee along with him, and he began to be sorrowful and troubled. 38 Then he said to them, "My soul is overwhelmed with sorrow to the point of death. Stay here and keep watch with me."

MEDITATION

Jesus knew without any doubt that the pressing of His life would produce the oil of salvation.

Write a prayer asking Yahweh to help you to not be fearful of the press. Without the press there is no oil.

Ylang Ylang

SPIRITUAL MEANING: The scent helps overcome fear and promotes self-confidence. Also means rare.

ORIGIN:

Ylang Ylang essential oil is native to countries such as India, the Philippines, Malaysia, Indonesia, and parts of Australia. Ylang Ylang's heady aromatic scent is fruity, flowery and rich. Ylang Ylang is extracted by steam distillation from fresh flowers of the Ylang Ylang tree.

BENEFITS:

Can be used as an antidepressant, antiseptic and sedative. It's also used to lower blood pressure and added to perfumes. Boosts hair strength and growth.

BLENDS WELL WITH:

Bergamot, Lemon, Sandalwood, Frankincense, Lavender, Patchouli and Wild Orange.

DIFFUSER BLENDS:

Relaxation & Sleep	Hope	On the Beach
3 drops Ylang Ylang	4 drops Bergamot	3 drops Patchouli
2 drops Lavender	3 drops Ylang Ylang	3 drops Wild Orange
2 drops Bergamot	2 drops Frankincense	2 drops Ylang Ylang

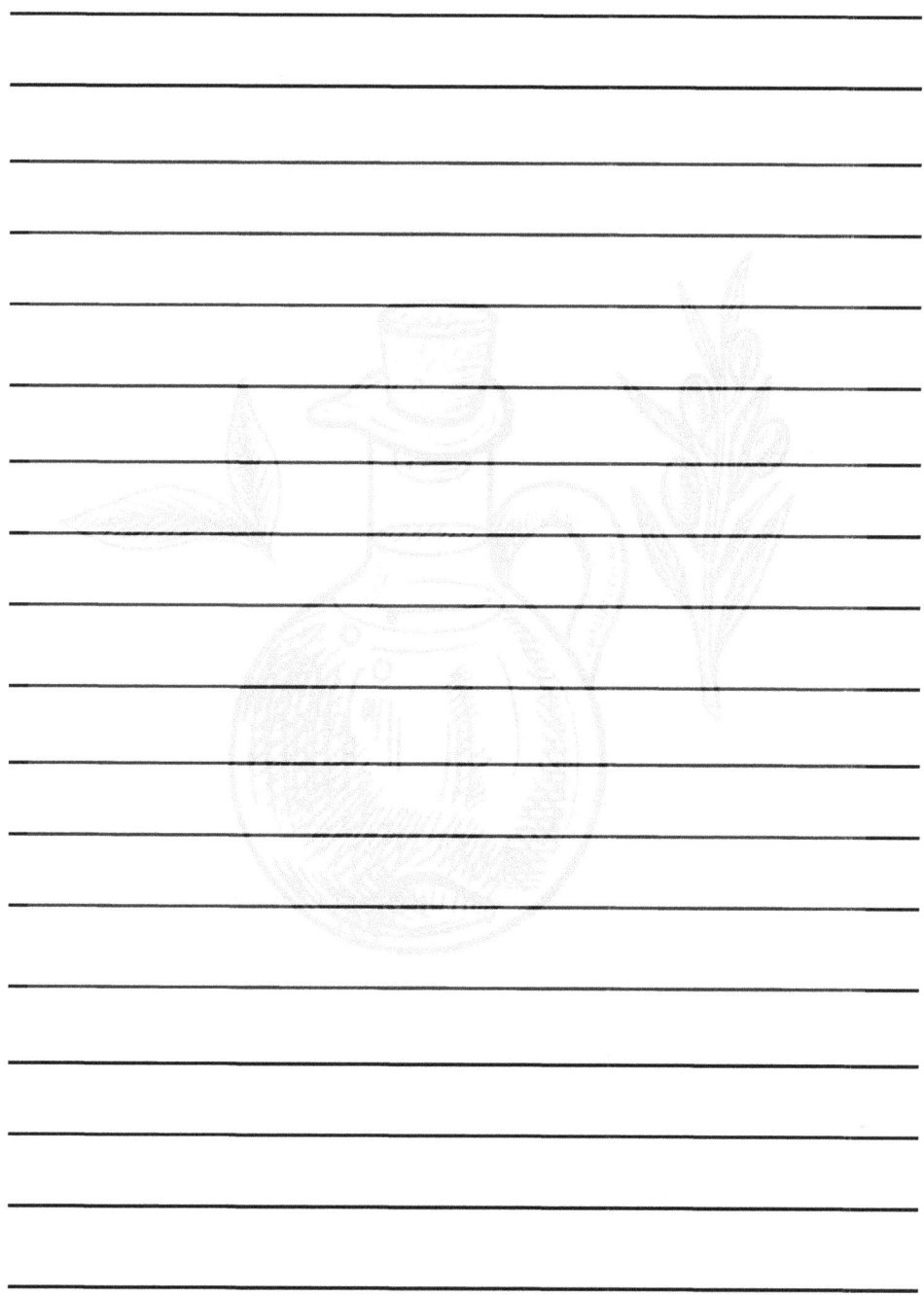

Extra Reflection Pages

_____

_____

_____

_____

_____

_____

_____

_____

_____

_____

_____

_____

_____

_____

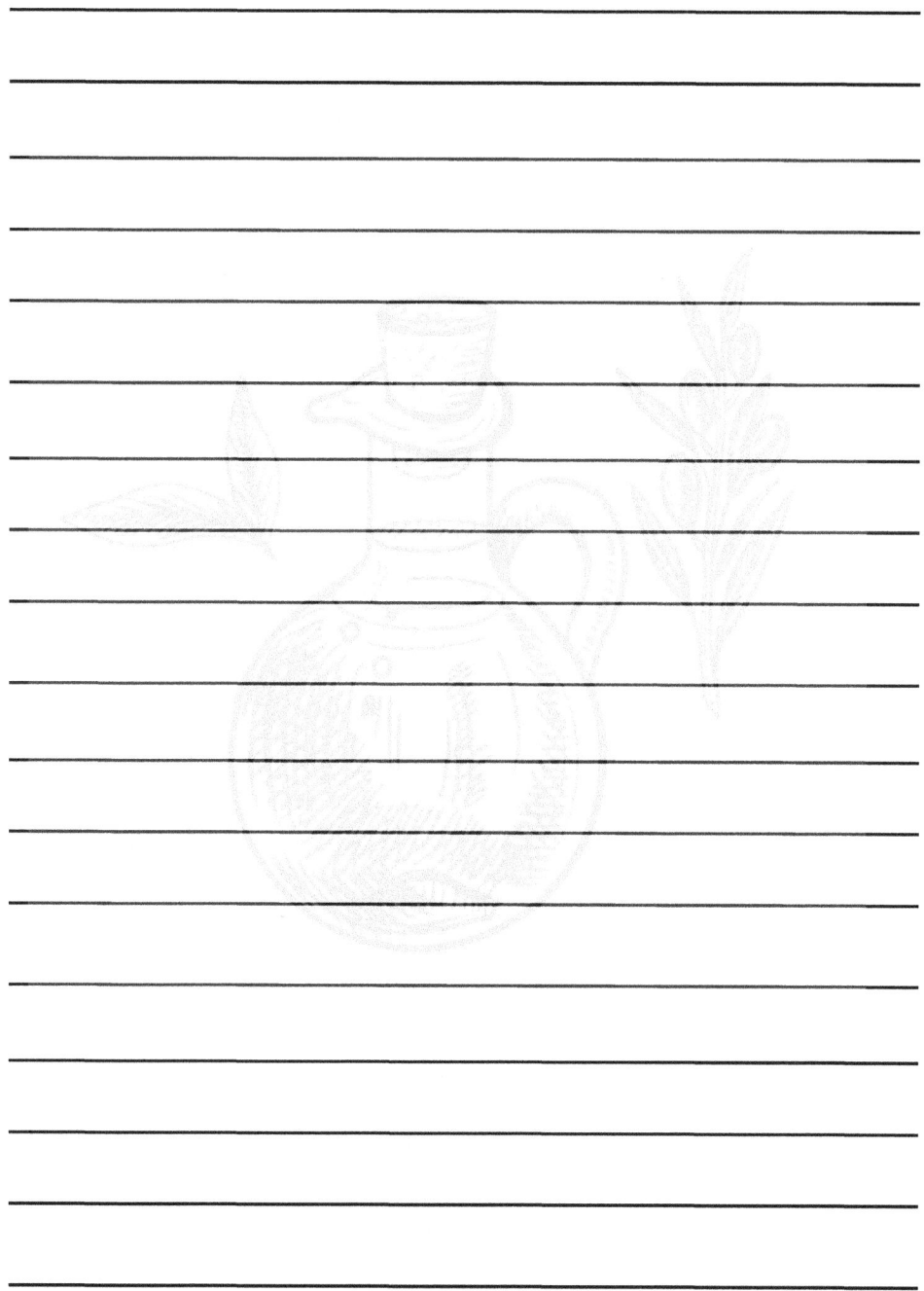

Extra Reflection Pages

_____

_____

_____

_____

_____

_____

_____

_____

_____

_____

_____

_____

_____

_____

Extra Reflection Pages

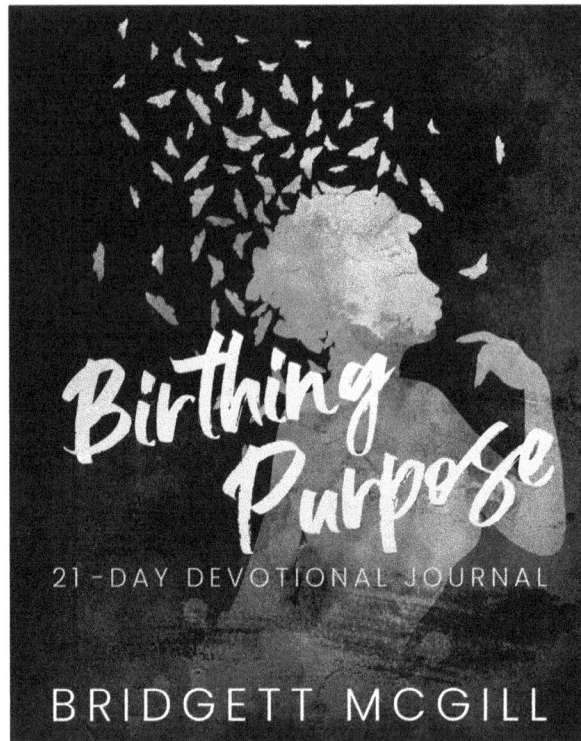

Mark Twain said "The two most important days in your life are the day you are born and the day you find out why."

How long have you been asking yourself the question "What is my purpose on this earth?" How long have you been trying to connect the dots and fill in the blanks? This journal is for every Beautiful and Divinely created WOMAN, who is gifted at birth with her purpose. No matter how long it takes her to see it, believe it and birth it, what she has inside her to bring forth is hers.

In the same way we can be pregnant physically, we can also be pregnant spiritually; with ideas, visions, inventions, projects, plans and the like.

Give yourself permission and be intentional in seeking your purpose. For 21 - days, allow yourself to explore hidden desires, tucked away dreams and plans unfulfilled. Don't be surprised at what you find within yourself; it's been there all the time. Get ready to walk in your purpose; the world is waiting for you.

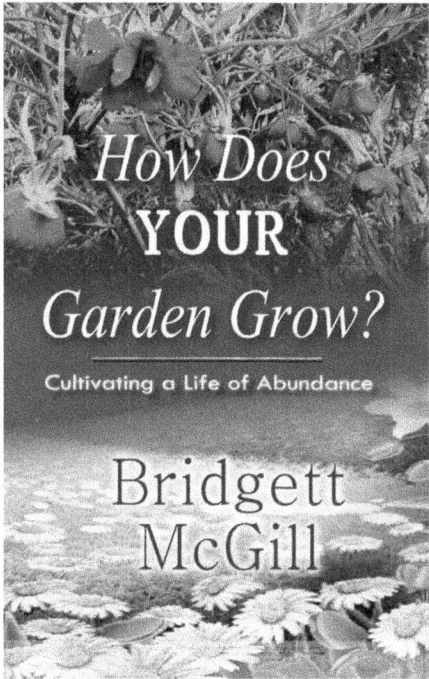

If you compared your life to a garden right now, right today, what would you find? Is it flourishing, lush and full; are there a few green spots here and some brown patches there, or is it depleted because you've given everything away? We have to ask ourselves every day; What does my garden need? Does it need the sun of encouragement; could it benefit from the fertilizer of forgiveness; would the pruning of confession bring great relief, or is it simply craving the beauty of rest?

As we walk through the gardens of our lives, we will find that we have within us all we need to cultivate a life of abundance; we only have to be still, listen and let the beauty come forth.

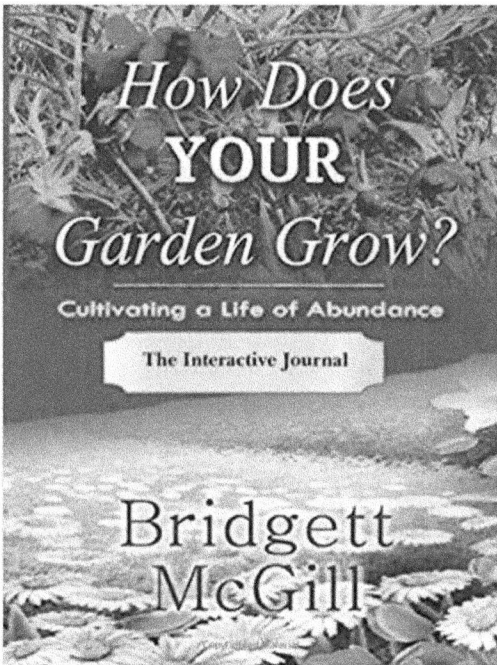

~~~~~~
~~~~~~
~~~~~~

How Does Your Garden Grow? Cultivating a Life of Abundance, Interactive Journal is an amazing tool to cultivate growth and healing. In this interactive journal, you will go beyond writing "What are you thinking and what are you feeling." This journal will challenge you to dig into your heart, pull up weeds of stagnation, fertilize your desires and sow into your creativity. This workbook, if you will, is filled with questions, challenges, prayers quotes, scriptural references for further biblical study and excerpts from the book *"How Does Your Garden Grow? Cultivating a Life of Abundance* by Bridgett McGill

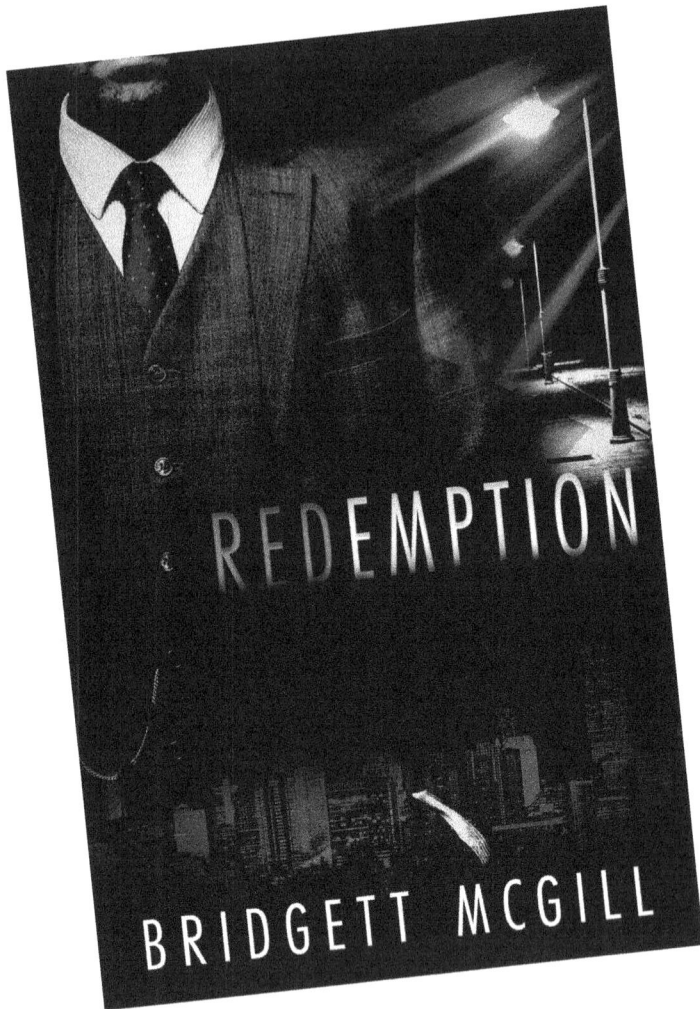

REDEMPTION

BRIDGETT MCGILL

Khalil Benson has taken on the biggest case of his legal career. His client pulled the trigger, but something else might be the cause of the victim's death. Pressure mounts as the media and public press for answers in a city cover-up. Khalil will need his street savvy gained from growing up on Chicago's Westside, and his experience winning cases that others considered lost causes, and a dedicated team, to unravel the threads of secrecy and betrayal to bring down a politically connected prosecutor and free his client.

Ava Penwood has settled in for the long haul after serving three of a thirty-five-year sentence, the aftermath of a night out that went horribly wrong. Until hope, packaged as a legal hotshot who has come into startling new information about her case, walks in with the promise of an appeal. Now she has to wrestle with her growing attraction for a man she barely knows and holds the balance of her life in his hands.

Facts or Fate … what will be true Redemption?

Bridgett McGill

is the award-winning author of How Does Your Garden Grow? Cultivating a Life of Abundance. She is the Founder of the women's empowerment organization, The Queen Within. She has loved writing since she was a child. A certified yoga instructor, she practices daily to enhance creative flow. She is an avid user of oils on her body, in her home and at work. She never leaves home without a bottle of oil in her purse. Chicago is home. She has two adult daughters and two grandchildren.

Sharon Gilchrist

is a woman of God on a spiritual journey toward her purpose. She is a believer in holistic living with the power of oils for her mind, body, and spirit.

She has been through some pressing in her life the last few years. This pressing and pouring has created a peace beyond understanding. It has created courage and confidence. She now knows that she is stronger than she thought she was!!!

"I have learned over the years that when one's mind is made up, this diminishes fear; knowing what must be done does away with fear."
Rosa Parks

www.ingramcontent.com/pod-product-compliance
Lightning Source LLC
Chambersburg PA
CBHW080601030426
42336CB00019B/3289